TAI CHÊN'S *Inquiry into Goodness*

Tai Chên's
Inquiry into Goodness

A TRANSLATION OF THE *Yüan Shan,*
WITH AN INTRODUCTORY ESSAY,
BY *Chung-ying Cheng*

EAST-WEST CENTER PRESS
Honolulu

To my parents

Contents

Preface

Tai Chên (1723–1777) is an important Chinese scholar and thinker of the Ch'ing period. His historical scholarship and critical methodology have frequently provoked zealous discussions in the forward-looking and progressive-minded intellectual circles in China since the time of the May Fourth Movement in 1919, but unfortunately much of his philosophical teachings remains unknown and unevaluated. The study of Tai Chên as a thinker and philosopher presented in this volume is not intended to be either exhaustive or complete. I have not tried to examine any of the Japanese studies on Tai Chên, for example, the justification being that I want my work to focus on an interpretation of Tai Chên's philosophy in the light of my knowledge of Chinese and Western philosophies, not on a textual and genetic examination of his writings.

In the past four decades, there have been a number of publications on Tai Chên. But perhaps with the exception of Hu Shih's *Tai Tung-yüan tê-chê-hsüeh* [Philosophy of Tai Tung-yüan], almost all of these publications approach Tai Chên from a textual or historical point of view; only a few aim at a philosophical elucidation and evaluation of his work. Even Hu Shih's work suffers from being overly concerned with the geneology of Tai Chên's thought and thus fails to bring out in bold relief Tai Chên's philosophical insights as viewed from a strictly philosophical point of view as well as from that of universal philosophical concepts.

This study is intended to be a philosophical study of Tai Chên's philosophy, centering about his concept of, and his explanation of his concept of, *shan* (goodness), an important Confucian idea; for it is this point—the development of the concept of *shan*—that determines Tai Chên's place in the history of the Confucian philosophy and a point through which we are able to ascertain his original contributions toward the persuasiveness of the Confucian doctrines.

This book consists of two parts: my introduction to Tai Chên's philosophical thought; and my English translation of Tai Chên's *Yüan Shan* [Inquiry into Goodness], one of his important philosophical treatises. The Introduction, titled "The Development of the Confucian Thought and Tai Chên's Philosophy of Goodness," is a philosophical— as opposed to the textual—as well as a critical—as opposed to the descriptive—explication of Tai Chên's ethical and metaphysical ideas in the context of Confucian philosophy. The translation, the first ever attempted in English and the main body of the book, is carefully done and is accompanied by detailed notes and annotations that show the cogent organization and the self-explanatory nature of the original essay.

My translation of Tai Chên's *Inquiry into Goodness* began in the fall of 1962, while I was a graduate student in philosophy at Harvard. Dr. Glen Baxter of the Harvard-Yenching Institute has taken great interest in my work ever since, and I am grateful to him for the unceasing encouragement he has given me. I wrote the introductory essay in the spring of 1965 at the University of Hawaii, where I started my teaching career in philosophy. During the past three years, my manuscript has been revised several times in the light of constructive criticisms received from my colleagues in Chinese studies. For the most compelling and revealing textual criticisms, I wish to acknowledge Professor Wang Chi-chen, former professor of Chinese at Columbia University, whose interest in having my translation of Tai Chên's *Inquiry into Goodness* published in *Monumenta Serica* I genuinely appreciated.

Professor Wing-tsit Chan has once urged me to translate Tai Chên's *Mêng Tzŭ tzŭ-yi shu-chêng* [Commentaries on the Meanings of Terms in the *Book of Mencius*], a larger and a better-known work by Tai Chên, a portion of which has been translated by Professor Chan himself in his book, *A Source Book in Chinese Philosophy*. I wish that I did have time to carry out this suggestion, for such an undertaking, I am sure, would definitely add great value to this volume. I hope that in the light of my present efforts in making a philosophical reconstruction of Chinese philosophy, I will have an opportunity in the future to reexamine Tai Chên's philosophy and other related Ch'ing philosophical writings that would enable me to achieve an understanding of greater precision, larger scope, and more penetrating depth.

Honolulu, Hawaii   Chung-ying Cheng
August, 1969

TAI CHÊN'S *Inquiry into Goodness*

Introduction: The Development of Confucian Thought and Tai Chên's Philosophy of Goodness

It has often been noted that there is more doctrinal homogeneity and continuity of thought in the development of Chinese philosophy than there is in Western philosophy. The main basis for this observation is that Confucianism seems to be the over-all pattern that characterizes Chinese thought as a whole, although it was eclipsed at times by the influences and appeal of Taoism from the second to the fourth century and by those of Buddhism from the third to the ninth century. Despite these periods of ascendancy of Taoism and Buddhism, Confucianism constituted the dominant school of thought and continued to grow.

That there have been marked differences within Confucianism at various times during various stages is not incompatible with the mainstream of Confucianism that is dynamic and dialectical. We may indeed relate all these differences to diverging attempts to interpret the ideas embodied in the Confucian Classics; or we may regard them as having been inspired by intervening challenges either from other schools of thought or from new circumstances and experiences in the society and culture.

It is unfortunate that many scholars of Chinese thought in their recent studies of Chinese Confucianism have not recognized the diverse and distinct aspects of Chinese Confucianism and therefore have tended to use the term "Confucianism" in multiple senses without distinguishing explicitly its references.[1] It is important that we be aware of the distinction between Confucianism as an ideology and an institutional practice in the traditional Chinese society since the time of the Former Han Dynasty, and Confucianism as a system of ethical and metaphysical ideas that has undergone many transformations and much development from the Classical period to the present. Confucianism in the former sense encompasses the teachings of, and practice in accordance with, the so-called Three Canons *(san-kang)*—concerning the rule of Heaven in relation to Earth, of father in relation to son, and of husband in relation to wife—and the Five Norms *(wu-lun)* —concerning the virtues between ruler and subject, father and son, elder and younger brother, husband and wife, and friend and friend. In this book, I shall not concern myself with a study of the development of Confucianism as an ideology or as an institution; rather, I shall confine myself to the development of Confucianism as a system of ethical and metaphysical ideas. I shall first give a brief account of the dialectical development of Confucian thought in the past. Then I shall try to show how Confucianism received an articulate formulation and elucidation, in the final stage of its development in traditional China, by Tai Chên, one of the leading Confucian scholar-thinkers.

THE FOUR STAGES IN THE DEVELOPMENT OF CONFUCIAN THOUGHT

There have been four stages in the development of Confucian thought that should command our attention. The first stage concerned the formulation of Classical Confucianism in the works of Confucius, Mencius, and Hsün Tzŭ. It was Confucius (551–479 B.C.) who first recognized the worthiness of man in his capacity to achieve self-perfection and the perfection of others and who described as *jên* the beginning and the utmost fulfillment of that capacity in a context of well-adjusted human relationships.

Since the concept of *jên* occupies a central position in the Confucian philosophy, I shall explain it in some detail. The significance of *jên* is manifold: in a broad sense it is the perfect virtue that comprehends all other virtues and is present in all other virtues. Thus in answer to Tzŭ Chang's question about *jên,* Confucius said: "To be able to practice five things everywhere under heaven constitutes *jên.*" These five things are "respectfulness," "tolerance (mindedness)," "sincerity," "earnestness," and "kindness" (*Analects* 17.6). In other words, *jên* is the defining characteristic of a good man or a superior man. Thus Confucius said, "If a superior man abandons *jên,* how can he fulfill the requirements of that name?" (*Analects* 4.5). "If a man be without *jên,* what has he to do with the rites of propriety? If a man be without *jên,* what has he to do with music?" (*Analects* 3.3).

Jên is also the continuum of goodness or virtue, which embraces all human beings as equal, but which is rooted in, and can grow in, every individual. Thus Confucius said: "Is *jên* a remote thing? If I wish to have *jên, jên* is at hand" (*Analects* 12.29). Again, he asserts: "Is anyone able for one day to apply his strength to virtue *(jên)*? I have not seen the case in which his strength would be insufficient" (*Analects* 4.6).

Finally, the principle of *jên* implies the obligation on the part of man to perfect and benefit others; in so doing, he will perfect and benefit himself. A man, therefore, can be seen in regard to his relationships with other men, even though he is also an irreducible individual entity with respect to other men and reality. Thus Confucius said, "Now the man of perfect virtue *(jên),* wishing to be established himself, seeks also to establish others; wishing to be enlarged himself, he seeks also to enlarge others" (*Analects* 6.30). In other words, Confucius, who considered man to be a combination of reason, desires, and feelings, all resulting from natural endowments, discovered the importance of leading a life guided by reason in which feelings and desires will fall into order. Such a life is a life of *jên,* and the realization of such a life is the realization of the potential of *jên* inherent in man.

When we come to Mencius (371–289 B.C.), we find that human nature is explicitly and directly identified with the capacities and the inherent tendencies of *jên* and other virtues. Mencius lamented that ordinary men do not recognize this and thus do not develop their original goodness. Thus he said: "*Jên* is man's mind, and righteousness is man's path. How lamentable is it to neglect the path and not pursue it, to lose this mind and not know to seek it again" (*Book of Mencius* 56.2). He argued that the tendency toward goodness in human nature is like the tendency in water to flow downwards. "There are none but have this tendency to goodness, just as all water flows downwards" (*Book of Mencius* 56.2).

The evidence of the goodness of human nature, according to Mencius, is found in some basic feelings of man—feelings that constitute the beginnings of virtues. Thus the "feeling of empathy" is the beginning of *jên*, the "feeling of shame and dislike" is the beginning of *yi* (righteousness), the "feeling of reverence" is the beginning of *li* (propriety), and the "feeling of approving and disapproving" is the beginning of *chih* (knowledge). On the basis of these, Mencius saw man as definitely capable of achieving perfection.

Believing in the goodness of human nature, Mencius was also able to argue for the possibility of realizing a well-ordered society and an established government by virtue on the basis of virtue. A government by virtue is one by which people enjoy well-being, justice, and harmony; it is one that has endurance. The principle of such a government, which Mencius stressed, is that a ruler should extend his likes to the people and should listen to the people. In other words, the ruler should develop his inherent goodness and let his goodness rule the people, who, through their own goodness, will be ruled. In view of this, a ruler's interests in profit, expansion of territory, and aggrandizement of power become quite extraneous, if not obstacles, to the establishment of a unified and harmonized state of well-being. Through his theory of the goodness of human nature, Mencius thus gave a new form and a new unity to the ethics and political philosophy of Confucius.

Hsün Tzŭ (fl. 298–238 B.C.), the last staunch Classical Confucianist, was no less great a pillar of Classical Confucianism than was Mencius, though often contrasted with him. His was a philosophy of social and cultural development and of the fulfillment of human reason. According to Hsün Tzŭ, human nature is bad in that the tendency toward self-indulgence and excess is stronger than is the tendency of self-control and moderation if an individual is left alone. This is due to the inherent nature of desires and emotions. But since desires and emotions are the life-materials of which man is made but of value only when their satisfaction and expression reach a point conforming to the dictates of reason, the development of human reason becomes important to Hsün Tzŭ. Human reason *(li)*,[2] according to Hsün Tzŭ, is a faculty of discerning and judging; it is at the same time a faculty of recognizing what is good and right from what is bad and wrong. But, said Hsün Tzŭ, since human intelligence may be considerably weaker in its power of control than are human desires or emotions, the development of an individual's reason (or intellect) must rely upon an objectified reasonableness that is expressed by social norms and ethical canons. In short, what Hsün Tzŭ posited as a check to the fallibility of human reason was the concept of propriety *(li)*, which, for Hsün Tzŭ, was the notion of social norms and ethical rules that always had applications to actual human relationships, because *li* in those days was founded and tested by the sage-kings to be conducive to peace, order, and the realization of human good. Thus Hsün Tzŭ held that individuals should try to conform to *li* in their conduct; and, moreover, that this conformity should not be passive but active, since it would be the beginning of active participation in a civic and social life from which individuals would derive satisfaction and through which they would achieve self-control.

Thus, Classical Confucianism, as expounded by Confucius, Mencius, and Hsün Tzŭ, did not condemn everything empirically known about human nature or human existence in and of itself; it did not deny or abnegate whatever that may add to the well-being and perfection of human beings, for all the Confucian virtues were meant to be products of the refinement and continuous cultivation of human nature, not a means of abolishing or absolving sin. Everything in the human experience was evaluated in terms of the over-all human existence of the whole and on many levels. Classical Confucianism, to be sure, affirmed that the whole had as much significance for an individual as the individual had for the whole, but this was not intended to be interpreted that the individual occupied a lesser place than the whole. This is obvious in the Confucian concept of *jên*: a concept that is intended to represent the ultimate balance and perfection that gives the utmost value both to an individual man and to the whole of humanity.

This view of human value and of its relation to the universe in Classical Confucianism was overshadowed in the second stage. For in this stage the primordial Confucian philosophy was somehow reshaped into a rigid but comprehensive system by Tung Chung-shu (197?–104? B.C.) and others of the Han Dynasty. Han Confucianism was a closed and stratified system of five agencies (*wu-hsing*) and two forces (*yin-yang*); it was pseudoscientific in the sense of being explanatory, even capable of providing predictions, but without being founded on experimentation; it also had the tendency to submit the value of man to a sequence of regulations viewed as inherent in Nature and to reduce the vitalistic and voluntaristic ideas in Classical Confucianism to some attenuated form of materialism and determinism. In spite of all such deviations and its cosmological elaborations, however, there were in Han Confucianism elements that were recognizeable as the Classical Confucian ideal of man's nature and its fulfillment. In fact, Han Confucianism never denied or renounced the following two important doctrines of Classical Confucianism: that the achieving of human self-perfection and perfection of others in the context of man's relationships conforms to the truth of Heaven and is an implicit consequence from the cosmological affirmation of the universal correlation of things and forces in the universe; and that human value be accepted as a balanced development of human capacities in terms of every aspect of human desires and emotions, since no evil is directly traced to the substantiality of the appetitive nature of man, but rather to the facts of maladjusted, uncultivated relationships or tendencies in man, whereas all good is traced to some intrinsic part of human capacity. All in all, in the second stage of Confucian development, there was no self-renunciation as such, since there was no renunciation of objective reality as being irrelevant to the achievement of good.

The third movement of Confucian thought was a reassertion of the basic themes of Confucianism that took place after Confucianism had survived the challenges and modifications from the widespread Buddhistic impact. Buddhism, from its very beginning, explicity contradicted the two fundamental doctrines of Classical Confucianism— the positive relevance of the whole to the achievement of goodness and the positive relevance of the value of every part of human nature to the achievement of goodness. Buddhism described the whole world as being completely subjective, and the subjective as leading only to suffering; hence, for the purpose of one's salvation and the salvation of all of humanity, Buddhism renounced both the objective world and the individual life processes. Confucianism had to meet the challenges of such a sophisticated metaphysical system; its ethical justification of human existence first had to be metaphysically vindicated. The ultimate objective being to refute Buddhism—whose sophistication it often respected—the reconstruction of Confucianism resulted inevitably in the metaphysical and cosmological speculations of the founders of Neo-Confucianism, Chou Tun-yi (1017–1073), Shao Yung (1011–1077), and Chang Tsai (1020–1077).

It should be natural for us to separate these earlier Neo-Confucianists from the later Neo-Confucianists of the period that began with the Ch'êng brothers—Ch'êng Hao

(1032–1085) and Ch'êng Yi (1033–1107)—and culminated in the system of Chu Hsi (1130–1200); and revitalized in the system of Wang Yang-ming (1472–1529). The earlier Neo-Confucianists were cosmologically minded. They were interested in finding the truth where truth was denied by the Buddhists. They wanted to be positivistic, relationalistic, and unifying. They were interested in seeing the world in order, harmony, and beauty, and in being continuous with the Way of Heaven. But in doing this, they tended to reassure the state of quiescence more than the state of active participation. It is difficult to say whether the earlier Neo-Confucianists, who contented themselves with this attitude, did so under the influence of some form of Taoism or Buddhism. But what is important is that they believed that this state enabled one to discover *li* (principle or reason) naturally. *Li* is the objective order, the harmony, and the beauty of things. *Li* is further conceived of as the guiding, regulating, controlling, and molding force or law inherent in everything. Through this formative regulation of *li*, man is enabled to recognize not only the unity of things but also the individuality of each thing, as is given to him, or as is possibly given to him.

In their use of the term "*li*," as described above, the Neo-Confucianists contrasted *li* with *ch'i* (the natural existence), of which *li* is the governing and organizing principle. *Ch'i* is theoretically separable from *li* but is never really separated from *li*. In terms of *li* and *ch'i*, human nature is again explainable and intelligible. *Li* is identified with the rational elements, and *ch'i* with the irrational elements. The world is conceived of as a system resulting from the interaction of *li* and *ch'i*, in contrast to the Buddhistic Nothingness *(k'ung)*. Since *ch'i* is theoretically devoid of *li*, *ch'i* is responsible for the disorder and corrupting tendencies in things and therefore for those in man.

The later Neo-Confucianists thus deviated from Classical Confucianism in two important respects: First, they completely objectified human reason into a nonhuman order of things; they made the function of human reason a product of an objective reason, while objective reason depended upon human reason (mind) to make its authority and truth manifest. In short, the well-known Neo-Confucian doctrine of the "investigation of things" *(kê-wu)* is ambiguous,[3] for there are no effective restrictions regarding how objective reason is recognized as human reason. It was suggested by Chu Hsi that when mind in its seriousness *(ching)* is directed toward external things, it would be able to grasp the truth of things. From this it is easy to see why Wang Yang-ming, following the thought of Lu Chiu-yüan (1139–1193), criticized Chu Hsi and why he himself naturally and logically (in the light of the difficulties of Chu Hsi's philosophy) took mind as the principal condition of knowledge and of truth. Thus, in the eyes of Wang Yang-ming, *li* as objective reason was, and had to be, subjectivized. He had then, on the one hand, the world as the changing creative unity preserved, whose development made possible by mind; and, on the other hand, the absolute authority and autonomy for an individual who claims to have realized *jên* and sincerity *(ch'êng)*— and therefore all truth—in his mind.

A second deviation concerned the status of human nature in relation to its ideal of perfection and development. According to Wang Yang-ming, the desires and emotions of an individual that lead to excesses and to the beclouding *(pi)*[4] of rational vision[5] are to be condemned as undesirable. He was of the view, moreover, that in harmony, which is a rational order, individual desires and emotions are totally trivial; and that, since it is quite possible for human beings to control, eliminate, and suppress their desires and emotions, these desires are to be subdued accordingly.

Thus, we are given, on the one hand, *ch'i*, as a necessary constituent in the formation of the cosmos, since desires are eliminated from rational sagehood; we are given, on the other hand, desires and emotions that are natural and that require an outlet. But no outlet is permitted under the authority of mind. Thus, it is not surprising that the extreme discipline of *li* of the Chu Hsi school finally led to the extreme eccentricity of "wildcat Ch'an" *(yeh-hu-ch'an)* of the late Wang Yang-ming school.[6]

The third movement in the development of Confucian thought, in terms of Neo-Confucian philosophy and in the light of the above characterization, may be considered, in one sense, to have been a reconstruction of Classical Confucianism; but, in another sense, the creation of a new philosophy and a new ideal, because it differed from Classical Confucianism in lacking open-texturedness and dynamic flexibility. In this stage, Confucianism was formalized into an ideal principle or order that only served to discipline and yet to restrict the proper development of human nature that was based on the rational intuition of goodness. Consequently, when circumstances in the social and cultural life changed, it failed to satisfy the needs of intellectual minds to act and organize accordingly.

What took place as the final and fourth development of Confucian philosophy was thus only natural, a development revolving around the critique made by the Ming-Ch'ing Confucianists, who, having experienced a dynastic collapse, wished to open a new front of thinking to protest and to rehabilitate the moral creative life of the nation. Indeed, the last stage of Confucian development was a critical one, because it was in this stage that serious criticism was launched against the orthodox Neo-Confucianism of both the Ch'êng-Chu school and the Lu-Wang school. It was a criticism reflecting the conscientious efforts of the Confucian scholar-thinkers in the last days of the Ming Dynasty who tried to save the intellectual sanity of the loose, stagnant intelligentsia; it was a voice of protest and defiance in the face of national crisis. Patriotic nationalism, democratic ideas, principles of unification on the basis of vitalism and voluntarism, and affirmations of values of pragmatic actions characterized the writings of such well-known seventeenth century Confucian scholar-thinkers as Ku Yen-wu (1613–1682), Wang Fu-chih (1619–1692), Huang Tsung-hsi (1610–1695), and Yen Yüan (1655–1704). These men were conscious of the pitfalls of the Sung-Ming Neo-Confucian systems that inclined man to be removed from the actual practice of goodness and therefore to be alienated from reality. Because goodness had become only an abstraction in the Neo-Confucian system, the Ming Ch'ing Confucianists, who wanted to restore the vitality of Confucian life, had to have goodness made a concrete reality in terms of creative force, individual practice, and true unity of understanding and action.

The Confucianists of the fourth stage thus gave a new interpretation to the dialectical and dynamic philosophy of change in the *Yi Ching* [Book of Changes]. I regret that space does not permit me to examine in detail here any one of the following: the dynamic and dialectical vitalism of Wang Fu-chih, whose originality and vigorous systematic expressions of an organic philosophy of *ch'i* deserve separate discussion; Huang Tsung-hsi's revealing and objective criticisms of despotism and his formulation of the historical ideas, and Yen Yüan's pragmatic vitalistic philosophy of human nature and action as a protest against both the Ch'êng-Chu and the Lu-Wang schools of Neo-Confucianism. These scholars were not only critics of the earlier Neo-Confucianism but also original thinkers who made contributions of their own,[7] the chief ones being that of abolishing the abstract notion of "goodness," as was upheld by Sung-Ming Neo-Confucianism, and that of proposing in its place a concrete notion of goodness in the contexts of social and individual life and the universe. This concrete idea of goodness, however, was not given an explicit, systematic, and comprehensive formulation and justification until more than one hundred years after Wang Fu-chih and Yen Yüan raised their voices against Sung-Ming Neo-Confucianism. That positive Confucian philosophy was formulated by Tai Chên, a Confucian scholar and a systematic thinker who represents the culmination of the movement against Neo-Confucianism.

From this point of view, Tai Chên can certainly be regarded as representing the constructive apex of the critical Confucianism of the Ming-Ch'ing Era; and his philosophy as capturing the essential characteristics of the fourth and final stage of traditional Confucian philosophy. The importance of Tai Chên and his philosophy in the whole process of evolution of Confucian thought, therefore, cannot be overlooked. The remainder of this book will be devoted to the discussion of the main aspects of Tai Chên's philosophy.

TAI CHÊN AS A CONFUCIAN PHILOSOPHER

Although Tai Chên had no direct contact with the surviving Ming Confucian scholars' struggle with Neo-Confucianism and with the suppressing forces of the newly founded Ch'ing Dynasty, he may be regarded, in both spirit and practice, as the true intellectual disciple of, and heir to, the earlier critical Neo-Confucianists. From a philosophical viewpoint, it is relatively unimportant to prove how Tai Chên derived his ideas from his educational background, as has been done by Hu Shih,[8] because there is nothing that is conclusive about it that a textual or biographical study can offer. More important than this, however, is the fact, evident both from the study of Tai Chên's criticisms of Neo-Confucianism and from his own philosophy, that he inherited the true spirit of the earlier critical Neo-Confucianists. His inductive and empirical study of the earlier texts of the Confucian Classics and other writings in connection with astronomy, hydrography, and phonology give ample evidence that he not only followed but also enlarged upon his predecessors' empirical methodology of textual investigation. What concerns us here, however, is his important contribution to the criticism of the Neo-Confucian system and, in the light of this, his contribution to the formulation of a positive Confucian philosophy.

Tai Chên was born in the town of Hsiu Ning in the province of An-hui in mid-Eastern China.[9] He came from a small merchant's family. In his youth he had been employed as a shop apprentice. When he was twenty years old, he studied under Chiang Yung (1681–1762), a scholar

famous for his textual criticisms based on phonology. At
the age of twenty-four, he published a book titled *K'ao-
kung-chi-t'u chu* [Commentary on the Diagrams of Tech-
nological Records], which made him reputed for his learning. In 1762 he passed the examination for the *chü-jên*
degree. Although he was unable to pass the examinations
for subsequent higher degrees, in 1773, he was recommended to the Court for a government position by a group of
distinguished scholars and was immediately appointed an
editor in the then well-known Library of the Four Treasur-
ies (Ssǔ K'u Ch'uan Shu Kuan).[10] He spared no effort in
writing and researching in the fields of phonology, astronomy, hydrography, textual criticism of the Classics, and
even applied trigonometry. He also seemed to have a zeal
for expressing his philosophical ideas, which are found in
his essays on goodness, change, natural law, and the problem
of human nature. After Tai Chên's death, his works (fifteen
out of some fifty works) were collected together into the
Tai-shih yi-shu [Remaining Works of Mr. Tai].[11]

Tai Chên's philosophical writings[12] are represented
by the following four works: *Fa-hsiang-lun* [Essays on Law
and Phenomena]; *Yüan Shan* [Inquiry into Goodness], in
three parts; *Ta P'êng chin-shih Yün-ch'u shu* [Reply in
Letter to P'êng Chin-shih]; *Mêng Tzǔ tzǔ-yi shu-chêng*
[Commentaries on the Meanings of Terms in the *Book of
Mencius*].

Tai Chên wrote the *Yüan Shan* [Inquiry into Good-
ness][13] in 1765, before he was forty-one years old. The first
version of it consists of only three short essays pertaining
to philosophical explanations that have no textual reference
to the Confucian Classics. It is said that Tai Chên was so
happy when he finished the first of these short works that
his taste for food became especially keen.[14] Between 1768
and 1774, Tai Chên expanded these three short works by
incorporating them with two other short ones on human
nature and the Confucian Classics: *Tu Yi Hsi-tz'ǔ lun-hsing*
[Reading the *Great Appendixes* on Nature in the *Book of
Changes*] and *Tu Mêng-tzǔ lun-hsing* [Reading about Nature

in the *Book of Mencius*]. These additions serve to confirm and illustrate the ideas he presented in the earlier three works, each of which Tai Chên amplified by relevant additions whereby each essay read four to five times its original in terms of length alone. He also wrote a brief preface to the whole work, which shows how he intends to expose the true teachings of the Classics and, in a systematic way, how much he has contributed to the clarification and interpretation of the Confucian philosophy.

The *Commentaries on the Meanings of Terms in the* Book of Mencius,[15] which is considered the most important of Tai Chên's works and whose original title was *Hsü Yen* [Prefatory Words], was written in 1768; it got its present title around 1774, though it was not published until after Tai Chên's death (1777). Tai Chên spoke of this work, about a month before his death, in a letter he wrote to Tuan Yü-ts'ai:

> The most significant major work I have written is the *Commentaries on the Meanings of Terms in the* Book of Mencius. It contains the essentials for rectifying the minds of the people. Nowadays, everybody, good or bad, always calls his own private opinions *li* (reason or principle) and therefore causes catastrophies to the people. That is the reason why I must write that commentary on the *Book of Mencius*.[16]

Obviously, Tai Chên intended his last work as a critique of the prevailing Neo-Confucian attitude and opinions.

Previous to writing his commentary on the *Book of Mencius,* Tai Chên, in 1777, wrote a letter, titled "Reply in Letter to P'êng Chin-shih," to refute the objections raised against his criticisms of Neo-Confucianism.

As shown in the discussion above, Tai Chên had two objectives in mind in writing his works: to criticize the Neo-Confucian notion of *li* (reason or principle); and to reconstruct the Classical Confucian notion of *shan* (goodness). Hence, a discussion of Tai Chên's philosophy should not neglect either one of them, and, in this regard, Tai Chên's *Inquiry into Goodness* becomes especially significant because in it are given Tai Chên's explanation and justification of his philosophical position.[17]

In the *Inquiry into Goodness,* moreover, is seen Tai Chên's most constructive aspect, as opposed to the critical as seen in his commentary on the *Book of Mencius*; more specifically, in this work is found Tai Chên's reconstruction of Confucianism in terms of the concept of *shan*, a dominant idea in Mencius that had since received no close examination or elaboration. Thus, in discussing Tai Chên's critique of the Neo-Confucian system, I shall emphasize his *Commentaries on the Meanings of Terms in the* Book of Mencius; but in discussing his constructive philosophy of goodness, I will pay special attention to his *Inquiry into Goodness*. It is important to remember, moreover, that it is in his elaborate analysis of the concept of goodness that the significance of his philosophy and the distinguishing characteristics of the fourth stage of Confucian development as a critical and constructive intellectual movement are found.

TAI CHÊN'S CRITIQUE OF NEO-CONFUCIANISM: METAPHYSICS

Tai Chên's critique of Neo-Confucianism can be discussed on two levels, the metaphysical and the ethical, although it is recognized that both are in a sense interdependent. On the metaphysical level, Tai Chên rejects the Neo-Confucian notion of reality in terms of *li* (principle or reason); on the ethical level, he rejects the Neo-Confucian bifurcation of human nature. I shall discuss the metaphysical level in this section; and the ethical, in the next.

I have already noted that, according to Neo-Confucian metaphysics, *li* is the universal principle, form, and structure of things. It not only constitutes the guiding spirit in human nature but also represents the truth and reality of it; in effect, *li* is associated with the rational part of human nature. Man knows *li* because *li* is clearly present in man's nature. The objectivity of *li* testifies to, and guarantees, the unity and uniformity of human nature. *Li*, therefore, is also the principle of virtue inherent in human nature. The rest that is found in human existence is non-*li*, which has nothing to do with virtue and which is not to be tolerated.

As *li* is thus conceived, the question arises how we can come to know *li*. That the mind *(hsin)* knows *li* naturally is one possibility; that the mind comes to know *li* through an investigation of things is another; the important point here is that both lead to the positing of *li* and to the subjective imposition of one's opinions. And it is precisely this point that Tai Chên spoke of when he said that the difficulty with the notion of *li* is that it cannot be conceived of in such an a priori and abstract way and that intrinsically there can be no universal way for settling disagreements concerning *li*; for the settlement of opinions concerning *li* will often rest with those who have authority or prestige or power. Any argument on the basis of *li* will finally lead to an argument by authority, as is often seen in men who have authority who either suppress the ideas of their opponents or justify their own vicious and intemperate acts in the name of *li*.

To be more specific, *li* will lead, on the one hand, to absolute inaction and quietude for the soft-minded; on the other, to absolute licentiousness and moral laxity for the strong-willed. Tai Chên noted therefore that actualities are sacrificed when *li* is considered separately from things and is identified instead with one's opinions.[18] An immediate consequence of this separation—*li* from things and reality —is that things will lose their useful value. In a political and social context, it means that the ruler and the ruling class will quickly do harm to the people; the ruler and ruling class, seeing themselves as embracing every *li*, see the ruled mass as an object of exploitation to be reprimanded should it fail to cater to their likings. The more the ruler governs by *li*, the more the people suffer by *li*. Moreover, because of the abstract and idealized nature of *li*, the ruler will take no guidance other than what appears to him to be *li*; he will not look into the true reality of life and concrete facts of human nature and will therefore close his eyes to the needs and feelings of the people. And even if he did open his eyes, he would only see evil in the feelings of people for this reason: he identifies them with what is contrary to what he would call *li*.

Tai Chên thus completely rejected the abstract and metaphysical concept of *li* in the Neo-Confucian philosophy as being not in accord with humanity and reality because it failed the tests of universal agreement in terms of the universal feelings of man. It must be recognized, affirmed Tai Chên, that the reality of human nature is its needs *(yü)* and feelings *(ch'ing)*, which are universal human traits. They are universally human because the use of reason without the recognition of the values of these traits will lead only to monstrosities to which man will react immediately with aversion. Human needs and feelings that define humanity have a metaphysical justification—they are derived from the universal life-material in the world that is intrinsically good.

Before discussing Tai Chên's metaphysical justification regarding human needs and feelings, I wish to point out that Tai Chên, in his rejection of the Neo-Confucian notion of *li* and in his affirmation of the universal needs and feelings of man, nowhere denied the existence and importance of *li,*. On the contrary, *li,* as a principle of reality and humanity, according to Tai Chên, should be rectified to assume the true Confucian sense.

Tai Chên, first of all understood *li* as being coextensive with human needs and feelings when they are properly satisfied and balanced in the social milieu. *Li* is not separable either from human needs and feelings or from the whole of the society of man. *Li* is the balanced manifestation of individual life in both its rational and emotive dimensions in a society and a community. In this sense, *li* is derived from the vital nature of man: *Li* is the disciplined and well-regulated expression of feelings and needs of man. *Li* is not just a faculty of pure reason or discernment apart from its reasonable use. *Li* should not, and cannot, be separated from its embodiment of universal needs and feelings if harmony and proper satisfaction of feelings and needs are to be obtained. *Li* must be conceived therefore as being consistent and coherent with its reasonable application. But "reasonable application of *li*" implies that *li* is to be found only in concrete life-forms and activities, such as needs and feelings.

Tai Chên's concept of *li* can be further explained in three ways: (1) *li* is the pattern of things and therefore is not apart from things; (2) *li* is the over-all comprehension and consideration of the human heart regarding human needs and feelings; (3) *li* is the function or faculty that enables man to recognize both these points—(1) and (2)—and therefore is related to *ch'i* (vital force), which is the discerning and guiding ability of the mind for achieving comprehensive goodness in oneself, society, and the universe as a whole.

Conceiving *li* as the pattern of things, Tai Chên proposed a concept of *li* that is highly individualistic and highly empirical, as discussed in the following. *Li* dwells in things and varies with things. It is open to man's observation, and its understanding and discovery depend on man's discernment and distinction. In other words, Tai Chên considered *li* as the name for what we can discern in things and distinguish in their minute details, which is why *li* is also called the principle of discernment as well as the patterning and the shaping of things. If we know how things differ from one another, we should know the distinguishing traits of these things, these being called the *li* of structuring.[19] When *li* is conceived of in this manner, we may discover *li* in an objective way by empirical observation and theoretical analysis to the extent and on the premise that, by nature, things are intelligible and our understanding is possible. Tai Chên suggested that "the *li* of things and affairs can be obtained only in an analysis and dissection of the minutiae of things"[20] and that "the ancient men take understanding *(li-chieh)* as a matter of analyzing into the patterning and lining of things."[21] This idea of determining or finding *li* is certainly a more definite and clearer statement of how we may investigate things than that found in the writings of Chu Hsi or Wang Yang-ming.

Tai Chên further considered *li* to be a result of the investigation of things by analysis after synthesis and by synthesis after analysis.[22] Of course, *li* in this sense is not devoid of a metaphysical basis. What Tai Chên is objecting to is Chu Hsi's saying that *li* originates in Heaven and resides in the mind. For Tai Chên, *li* always dwells within things themselves; and what he seeks is the understanding of things. All things follow natural principles of their existence. But these natural principles of existence *(tzŭ-jan)* are necessary principles *(pi-jan)* to our understanding. Moreover, since everything has its natural principle of existence, there should be no a priori imposition made on things—imposition that is our mind's arbitrary interpretations of things. This is the reason, said Tai Chên, why we need an open mind for understanding the variety of *li* in a variety of things. Once we know the variety of *li* in a variety of things, we would obtain insights into the nature of things of various kinds; and, on this basis, we would be able to make predictions and universal generalizations.

Tai Chên anticipated a possible objection to his view in the light of the following saying by Mencius: "What the mind shares in common *(hsin-chih-suo-t'ung-jan)* is called *li* and *yi* (propriety and righteousness); it is the sage who acquires the knowledge of what the mind shares in common with every man."[23] The objection is that *li* can be localized in mind *(hsin)*. Although Tai Chên agreed with this statement by Mencius, he saw no reason why the conclusion that mind is *li* or *li* is mind should be drawn from it, as the Neo-Confucianists of the Lu-Wang school appeared to have done. For Tai Chên, the very important point about Mencius' saying lay in the phrase "to share in common." The mind is not denied the function or ability of discerning *li*. But because the mind can be mistaken in its discernment, there is a need for a check and test in universal agreement and universal application. If what mind finds to be *li* is not universally applicable or agreeable, then that so-called *li* is merely opinion *(yi-chien)*. We should not justify the objectivity of *li* simply in terms of the functioning of mind; i.e., its judging and distinguishing activities. The mind can know *li*, and it can judge the rightness or wrongness of a representation of *li*. But only when the true knowledge of *li* is ascertained can *li* be considered as *yi*. That *yi* is *li* is known only by a conscious mind; thus it is important that we should keep unhampered the faculties of the mind of distinguishing and judging. Only then will there be no beclouding in our conception of things and no ambiguities or prejudices in our understanding of things. (Tai Chên's explanation of the beclouding of mind will be discussed later in connection with his explanation of the selfishness of desires.)

Concerning the objectivity of *li* in concrete things and the rationality of mind as being capable of knowing *li*, Tai Chên believes that mind is not separate from the life-materials of which we are made. Mind and intelligence are only the subtle and refined parts of our natural existence. The activity of mind—thinking—is the subtle and refined part of mind. In all living things, according to Tai Chên, there exist refined and subtle parts, refined and subtle in different degrees and on different levels. Even within the order of man, there is the difference between the intelligent and the obtuse. But this fact does not affect the objectivity of *li*. Mind knows *li* only in the light of learning and discerning. The more learning and investigation a mind receives, the more *li* it will discern in things. But to say so is not to confuse *li* with mind or with the nature of human beings, as the Neo-Confucianists do.

TAI CHÊN'S CRITIQUE OF NEO-CONFUCIANISM: ETHICS

Since on a metaphysical level *li*, according to Tai Chên, is nothing other than patterns and organizations inherent in concrete things and revealed by cognitive capacities, *li* should consequently be found in human feelings and needs in that these represent concrete facts in life. In fact, *li* is the internal ordering and balancing of feelings and desires that contribute or lead to the over-all goodness and well-being of an individual in all his relationships with other individuals. As such, feelings and desires need to pass the test of universal agreement and universal application for their justification.

The feelings and desires of an individual are not intrinsically bad. On the contrary, metaphysically speaking, they are intrinsically good, because, as we shall see, they come from the life-materials that compose the whole universe. Evil stems from the extrinsic misplacing of feelings and desires. In other words, evil comes from the failure to pass the test of universal agreement and universal application in the development and satisfaction of feelings and desires. Because human desires and feelings are intrinsically good, they are the true foundation of virtue; because the development and satisfaction of an individual's feelings and desires can be bad and evil, in the sense of hindering the natural development and satisfaction of the feelings and desires of other men, the development of intrinsic goodness needs restriction and modification through extrinsic relationships. Only within the restricting and modifying conditions of the larger context of all men's feelings and desires can a single individual's feelings and desires be justified fully and significantly. *Li* is precisely the function of developing and fulfilling an individual's feelings and desires in the light of, and in consistency with, the over-all comprehension and consideration of the development of the feelings and desires of other human beings. Thus, *li* is the recognized justification of the value of individual needs and feelings in terms of the values of social and universal harmony and well-being.

In the light of the understanding of *li*, as discussed above, Tai Chên's criticism of Neo-Confucian ethics is simple and pertinent: the Neo-Confucianists locate the *li* of virtue and human nature in places other than in feelings and desires. Thus, after they denounce feelings and desires as being totally devoid of *li*, they have no basis for justifying ethical principles other than their arbitrary opinions, which, as discussed earlier, only serve to impoverish an individual's life. For Tai Chên, *li* was nothing but the appropriateness of human feelings and desires and the harmony of all men in the developments of their feelings and desires. Thus he proclaimed:

> *Li* is the ordering of feelings without amissness. There is never a case where *li* obtains where feelings do not obtain. Whenever we do something to others, we should ask ourselves and meditate deeply: "If other men do this to me, can I take it?" Whenever we blame someone for something, we should ask ourselves and meditate deeply: "If another man does this to me, will I consider it just?" *Li* becomes clear to one when he thinks of other men in terms of himself. The so-called heavenly principle means the natural ordering and patterning inherent in things. We shall be able to do justice to the natural ordering and patterning inherent in things if we only think of others' feelings in the light of our own feelings.[24]

To think of others' feelings in the light of one's own feelings is the Confucian principle of not doing anything to others that we do not wish to be done to ourselves. It is the formal requirement of virtues and principles; it is the formal restriction that we should apply to the development of our feelings and desires, whereas development of feelings and desires in accordance with the formal requirement or restriction is the material principle of all our virtues. Tai Chên's criticisms of Neo-Confucian ethics were that the Neo-Confucianists failed to see the significance of the material condition of virtues and that they failed to formulate the formal condition of virtues that applied to that material condition of virtues.

If the feelings are the material foundation of moral virtues in terms of *li*, then the term "feelings" has a use, regardless of whether the formal condition is present. But the term "*li*" has a use only when the formal condition is obtained. To say that the formal condition of virtue is obtained is to say that the feelings, as they are developed, are harmonized. It may be conveniently suggested that feelings, when appropriately cultivated, are examples of concrete reasonableness, which should be defined as *li*. The various virtues are defined only in the actual contexts of appropriate development of feelings. Hence, *jên* is the comprehension of feelings in their appropriate use;[25] and *li* is called *yi* (righteousness), being shared in common by all things.

The test of universal agreement and universal application was criticized by Hu Shih as being misleading on the grounds that the individual who thinks of others' feelings in terms of his own may project his own feelings into others.[26] This is a plausible criticism only when one fails to see the open-texturedness of this test. Nothing can guarantee the absolute desirability of a certain feeling and action. But continuous and consistent use of the test of universal agreement and universal application should gradually bring goodness to full realization, because, over a period of time, one's intelligence becomes refined and one's understanding and experience increase. It is only in this context of learning that has a vision of comprehensive goodness (or *summum bonum*) that the test of universal agreement and of universal application can be seen to be the most rewarding and most appropriate method of establishing value-claims and, for that matter, genuine values of morality or virtues.

The discussion given above has shown how Tai Chên had proceeded from his criticism of the metaphysical notion of *li*, as the source of existence, to his criticism of the ethical notion of *li*, as the source of morality; and how the latter is implicit in the former; and how the former is elaborated in the latter. This leaves one more question to be answered in Tai Chên's critique of Neo-Confucianism: the question of the status of *yü*, or desires, in an individual's life.

The Neo-Confucianists condemned desires and therefore recommended the elimination of desires in man: *Wu-yü,* or desirelessness, was their goal of a rational life.

But how can one achieve that status of desirelessness? This question immediately leads to the method of achieving tranquility, reverence, or seriousness.[27] Even though Tai Chên did admit that the Neo-Confucianists had frequently made efforts to break down the quietist philosophy of the Taoists and Buddhists, he also said that he still recognized the quietistic tendencies in the Neo-Confucian philosophy, which the Neo-Confucianists concealed, though perhaps unconsciously, under their Confucian outlook. Tai Chên pointed out as an instance of these tendencies Chou Tun-yi's doctrine that unity of mind (nature) is desirelessness.[28] Tai Chên argued: to be desireless is to forego all actions of life and to forego self-cultivating activities; how then may we realize *li* in this respect? He also criticized the Neo-Confucianists' statement that "anything if is not done from *li* must be done from *yü,* if is not done from *yü,* is done from *li.*"[29] This statement is meant to eliminate *yü* and therefore encourage a useful and truly virtuous life. But Tai Chên objected to its implication—the exclusive duality of *li* and *yü*—as a most unrealistic appraisal of the functioning of human nature.

In his discussion concerning *t'ien-tao* (the way of heaven), *hsing* (nature), *ts'ai* (ability), *tao* (the way), and *ch'uan* (moral deliberations),[30] Tai Chên clarified how the Neo-Confucianists from the Ch'êng-Chu school to the Lu-Wang school separated *li* from things within shapes, partly because of their objection to the Buddhistic idealism of mere consciousness, but, ironically enough, also because of the influence of the Buddhistic idealism of mere consciousness.[31] Tai Chên made a particularly interesting observation that the Neo-Confucianists always justified their ideas by identifying them with the Classical Confucianist philosophy, particularly that of Mencius. But he asserted that this association could not be farther from the truth. The concepts of nature as *li* and mind as *li,* of *li* as the way of heaven, and of *li* as the power and ultimate principle of life are nowhere found in—or even fit in with—Tai Chên's understanding of the true doctrines of Confucius and Mencius. The

Classical Confucianists did not separate *jên* from things in life; they did not speak of oneness of mind; and they did not conceive of *li* as the guiding principle of life without reference to concrete things. In fact, the Classical Confucianists, such as Mencius, regarded only the following of the principles of righteousness and propriety as the ultimate goal of a virtuous life; and they treasured the nonselfishness of one's desires, not a state of tranquility and desirelessness, as the prerequisite for the perfecting of humanity. In short, to the Classical Confucianists, there was no abstract *li* apart from the concrete facts of a moral life.

In the case of Mencius, human nature, including all its natural inclinations and capacities, was conceived of as innately good. Nature is the nature of inclinations and capacities *(ts'ai)*; there is no other nature than this. But how sharply this is contrasted with the sayings of Chou Tun-yi, Ch'êng Yi, and Chu Hsi! All of these Neo-Confucianists took *ts'ai* as bad or as the cause of evil because they identified *ts'ai* with *ch'i* (vital force), which is completely devoid of *li*. Thus Chang Tsai said:

> Only after having forms do we have the nature of inclinations; but if we go back to the original, thus beyond the nature of inclinations, we will find the nature of Heaven and Earth (which is *li*). Therefore, a superior man has something different in his nature than just the nature of inclinations.[32]

Following the steps of Chang Tsai, Ch'êng Yi stated:

> If we talk only of *hsing* (nature) but do not talk of *ch'i* (vital force), our talk is not complete; but if we talk of *ch'i* but do not talk of *hsing*, our talk is not clear.[33]

Chu Hsi, pursuing this hint further, criticized Mencius as talking only of *hsing*, but not of *ch'i* and identified the causes of this omission to the influences of Hsün Tzŭ and Yang Chu.

Tai Chên carefully pointed out that Mencius' notion of *hsing*, which is good, is the same *hsing* we find in the activities of sense perception. According to Tai Chên,

Ch'êng Yi and Chu Hsi were the first of those who thought that *li* was first identified with Mencius' concept of good nature; at the same time, they identified with *ch'i* both Kao Tzŭ's notion of nature as life and Confucius' notion of nature as what men share in common. But this is a false picture of both Mencius and Kao Tzŭ, said Tai Chên, because neither has made a bifurcation of nature into *li* and *ch'i*. As noted earlier, the *hsing* of Mencius is the whole body of inclinations of life in an individual as is Kao Tzŭ's notion of nature as what is naturally given in human existence. But the difference between Kao Tzŭ and Mencius lies in this: Whereas Mencius thinks that human nature can be, and therefore should be, developed into full goodness because it is innately good and because it contains the beginnings of goodness, Kao Tzŭ thinks that man should preserve his natural bent and should not impose restrictions on his nature, because, being a Taoist, Kao Tzŭ regards virtue as being quite extrinsic to human nature.

Thus, according to Tai Chên, it is Hsün Tzŭ and Kao Tzŭ that the Neo-Confucianists actually approximate and could even appeal to for justification of their ideas in spite of their differences from, and criticisms toward, Hsün Tzŭ and Kao Tzŭ. Concerning Hsün Tzŭ, Tai Chên gave the following explanation: Hsün Tzŭ believes that human nature is bad, because he does not see virtue and righteousness as naturally inherent in the nature of man; thus, he advocates learning and cultivation in terms of the rules of propriety to guard against the bad tendencies in man and to maintain social order. The Neo-Confucianists such as Ch'êng Yi and Chu Hsi asserted, on the one hand, that human nature is good in that it has principles of righteousness and reason *(yi-li)* but, on the other hand, that it is bad in that it is also associated with the natural endowment *(ch'i-chih)*. This distinction between *yi-li* and *ch'i-chih* in human nature certainly in part overlaps with Hsün Tzŭ's doctrine that human nature is bad. To the extent that human nature has bad elements, such as *ch'i-chih,* human

nature is bad. Ch'êng Yi and Chu Hsi thus affirmed explicitly that badness must be recognized as part of human nature.

Kao Tzǔ's doctrine, as opposed to Mencius', is that
whatever is given in life is nature. But "whatever is given
in life" is taken by Kao Tzǔ to be nothing other than those
feelings and desires that pertain to survival and reproduction; hence, *yi* and *li* are precluded. Thus he would have
agreed with Hsün Tzǔ in seeing no existential connection
between human inclinations, on the one hand, and virtue
and righteousness, on the other. Unlike Hsün Tzǔ, however,
Kao Tzǔ affirmed that human nature is neither good nor
bad in any moral sense, but that man can be either morally
good or bad, and finally that true goodness resides in preserving one's natural capacity and spirit in a state of tranquility. This doctrine is implied in Ch'êng Yi and Chu
Hsi's view that man's nature can be either morally good
(as a result of *yi-li*) or morally bad (stemming from *ch'i-
chih*). Both Ch'êng Yi and Chu Hsi also made a distinction
between the pure nature of man in a state of tranquility,
which is *li*, and the actual human life, which participates in
natural endowments *(ch'i-ping)* and which therefore may
lead to evil. The purpose of making such a distinction was
to provide a basis for leading an ascetic life—a life eventual-
ly devoid of desires and feelings and completely restored to
the purity of *li*. This philosophical attitude is again not too
far from Kao Tzǔ's doctrine of treasuring the naturalness
and of preserving metaphysical goodness. The same
arguments apply to the ideas of the Lu-Wang school,
because the idealistic Neo-Confucianists held the view that
the mind is originally complete in itself; hence, that the
way to leading a sagely life is to restore the original mind
by abolishing all human desires.[34]

In sum: Tai Chên's critique of Neo-Confucianism
comprised primarily his wish to restore the original
meanings of the Confucian terms that had been misused
in the Neo-Confucian systems of philosophy. The Neo-
Confucianists had used such Confucian words as *t'ien-tao*,
jên, *li*, *hsin*, *hsing*, *ch'ing*, *yü*, *ch'üan*, and *ch'êng* in their

writings, but they had given these words different meanings
—meanings that they had unconsciously derived from the
Taoists and Buddhists or meanings that could be theoretically assimilated to the Buddhist and Taoist doctrines
and to the heterodox ideas of Hsün Tzŭ and Kao Tzŭ. Tai
Chên wanted to render what belonged to genuine Confucianism to Confucianism; and what belonged to Buddhism
and Taoism to Buddhism and Taoism.[35] He wanted to
restore the Classical Confucianism of the *Analects,* the
Book of Mencius, the *Li Chi* [Record of Rites], and the
Book of Changes. Their restoration may be disputed were
it to be understood in a literal sense; if, however, the restoration were to be understood as an attempt to reconstruct
and reinterpret Classical Confucianism in the spirit of
Confucius, Mencius, and other authors of the Classical
Confucian writings, I cannot but admire Tai Chên's ingenuity and his original contribution to Confucian thought.

TAI CHÊN'S PHILOSOPHY OF GOODNESS

I shall now discuss the systematic phase of Tai
Chên's Confucian philosophy, which stems from his critique
of Neo-Confucianism and from his close understanding of
Classical Confucianism. His philosophy may be entitled
a "philosophy of goodness," for, as will be shown, Tai
Chên's unique contribution to Confucian philosophy in its
dynamic and dialectical development lies in his comprehensive notion of goodness in both metaphysics and ethics.

Because the systematic aspect of Tai Chên's philosophy is closely related to his criticism of Neo-Confucianism, it is difficult to say which of the two has priority within
his philosophy. Theoretically, the criticisms should lead to,
and presuppose, a philosophy such as the one Tai Chên
proposed; and his philosophy of goodness amply justifies,
and should give rise to, his apt criticisms of Neo-Confucianism. In terms of temporal sequence, however, it
seems that Tai Chên had an earlier concern with genuine
philosophical observations, apart from his criticisms of

Neo-Confucianism; thus, his early work, *Inquiry into Goodness,* which contains no explicit criticisms of Neo-Confucianism, preceded his critical philosophy. Furthermore, three of his early short works[36]—*On Law and Phenomena, Reading the* Great Appendixes *on Nature in the* Book of Changes, and *Reading about Nature in the* Book of Mencius—already contained metaphysical and cosmological explanations of things and of their nature and function in the world—metaphysical and cosmological explanations that seem to epitomize the systematic presentations of his philosophy of goodness in his *Inquiry into Goodness.* For it is in this work that the notion of *shan* (goodness) is given as the over-all source and pattern of things. My discussion of Tai Chên's philosophy therefore will be based upon his writings mentioned above, together with the relevant passages from his *Commentaries on the Meanings of the Terms in the* Book of Mencius. I shall focus on how, in his *Inquiry into Goodness,* Tai Chên synthesized and systematized his ideas into a philosophy of goodness.

THE THREE FUNCTIONS OF *Tao* AND *T'ien*

Following the tradition of the *Book of Changes,* Tai Chên conceived reality in terms of the productive (creative) and the reproductive activities of *Tao* (The Way), which is nothing other than the process of formation and transformation we constantly observe in the change of things. Tai Chên explained *Tao* thus: "*Tao* is the same as the going and undergoing [of things]; [it is] the ceaseless creative production and reproduction of life. That is why *Tao* is called *Tao.*"[37] But *Tao* can be further conceived of as the interchange of the mutually complementary forces, the *yin* (the feminine) and the *yang* (the masculine). And Tai Chên fully accepted this idea as he did that from the *Great Appendixes* of the *Book of Changes:* that "the interchange of *yin* and *yang* is called *Tao*—what inherits [formation and transformation] is due to goodness; what accomplishes [things] is due to nature." Both goodness and naturalness are characteristics of *Tao*; they simply indicate functions and operations of *Tao* in its creative movement. Two principles are given regarding *Tao*: (1) that the ceaseless productive (creative) and reproductive activity of things *(shêng-shêng)* is *Tao* and is therefore the interchange of the *yin* and *yang*; (2) that the ceaseless creative activity of *Tao* has its internal ordering and patterning. Thus *Tao* has a function of ordering and patterning things *(t'iao-li)*; it therefore gives rise to the ordering and harmony in things and their change, through which the sage apprehends and discerns the creative and the harmonizing (or ordering) activities of *Tao*, or the interchange of the *yin* and *yang*. Tai Chên explained this idea thus:

> Heaven has the sun and the moon; the earth has rivers and mountains. The ordering of man, on the other hand, begins with the distinction between the male and the female and with the union of husband and wife. It is thus that the principles of the *yin* and *yang* are discovered. The sky forms itself by having an essential distinction between the sun and the moon; the earth forms itself by creating a natural meeting of mountains and rivers. The sun and the moon are the male and female principles that form worldly phenomena; the mountains and rivers are the male and female principles in the transformation of vital forces *(ch'i)*. But when we consider the *yin* and *yang* with respect to an individual person, we refer to the male and the female in flesh and blood.[38]

According to Tai Chên, *Tao,* besides having the functions of creative activity and ordering, is further distinguished by its function of "naturing" things, that is, by making things what they are. That things become what they are is due to the further differentiations of the *yin* and *yang* into the so-called five agencies—water, fire, wood, metal, and earth—a doctrine that first appears in the *Shu Ching* [Book of Documents].

The five agencies are called *hsing* (nature), the same word used by Tai Chên to describe *Tao*. Tai Chên asserted that the *yin-yang* comprehends the five agencies just as the five agencies comprehend the *yin* and *yang*. It is because of the various forms of distribution that the five agencies and the *yin* and *yang* take that things become what they are. On the one hand, things have their individual natures that have their own unity; on the other hand, these individual natures are derived from, and therefore participate in, *Tao* —the *yin* and *yang* and the elemental differentiations of *yin* and *yang* in terms of the five agencies. That *Tao* has the power of individualizing things can be taken as one of its important characteristics. Given such an understanding, it is readily seen why there are individual things and individual men: individual things and individual men are different from each other because they have different distributions of *Tao*.

The essential point that Tai Chên wanted to make is that nature (individualizing nature) is due to *Tao* or the *Tao* of Heaven and that the individual natures of things and men are describable in terms of their vital forces and their refined existence—mind and intelligence. Tai Chên regarded these vital forces and refined existence as the substance of individual natures, whereas he regarded the *yin-yang* and the five agencies as the substance of *Tao*, even though it should be noted that the substance of individual nature is but the individualizing distribution of the substance of *Tao*. In order to combine this individualizing function of *Tao* with its creative and ordering functions, the sense in which Tai Chên spoke of *shan* (goodness) should be noted: *shan* as the great thing shared in common by all things in the world. *Tao* gives rise to everything; *Tao* individualizes everything as everything; and, finally, *Tao* orders and harmonizes everything with everything else—all these are connoted in the use of the term "goodness." Thus, Tai Chên said:

> . . . goodness is used to mean what is inherent in man [and things]. That which man has and acts upon is due to his nature and which in turn forms their basis. The so-called

goodness is nothing other than the formation and transformation of Heaven and Earth and the function and capacities of nature. To know these should enable us to know
goodness.[39]

Because all things in the world, including men, are
created, individualized, and ordered by *Tao*, different as
they are, they still possess something in common. As desires
(yü) and perceptive abilities *(chüeh)* constitute parts of the
nature of things, the animal beings and men share the same
desires and perceptive abilities. But to say this, according
to Tai Chên, is not to ignore the distinction between men
and things. Things have small endowments from *Tao* and
remain as things, whereas man takes great endowments
from *Tao* and therefore becomes man. These natural
endowments are called natural inclinations *(ts'ai)* or natural
qualities *(ts'ai-chih)*. *Ts'ai-chih* are the exhibition of nature,
or better, of the configurations of nature. For instance, gold
has its natural qualities that are different from those of
tinsel. But even within the same class of things, differences
may be seen in their qualities in terms of degrees of crudeness and refinedness. From the point of view of the thing
itself, what makes a thing specialized in its own way is its
nature; but from the point of view of the comprehensive
Tao, the same may be attributed to necessity *(ming)*. In
other words, things can be defined either in terms of its
natural qualities or in terms of its relation to *Tao* when its
natural qualities are formed—that relation being called
necessity (ming); hence, it can be said that *nature* and *necessity* are merely two different aspects of things,[40] the internal
and the external aspects. It then can be said that things differ
- from men because they have different necessities from *Tao*
and therefore possess different natures that exhibit themselves in their natural inclinations. The individualizing
power of *Tao* can therefore be called the power that gives
both nature and necessity to things and, hence, the power
that lays down the natural qualities of things for the things
themselves and for their relationships with other things.

THE NATURE AND NATURAL INCLINATIONS OF MAN

The analogy that different metals have different natural qualities applies to the class of things called men. Men have the same kind of natural endowments from *Tao*, which forms their nature. Analytically speaking, man has nature, natural inclinations, and necessity, all three referring to the same reality. The nature of man comprehends the complete capacities of Heaven and Earth. That is, as Tai Chên saw it in the genuine spirit of Confucianism, man in his complete nature partakes of every power and quality of *Tao* and, therefore, is not separated from *Tao*. Man is a plenum of *Tao*, though in a potential form. Nothing is deficient in him, though it is true that individual men may differ in their possession of natural qualities in terms of degrees of crudeness and refinedness, this being due to necessity. Man is capable of comprehending *Tao* because he has mind and intelligence that are caused by *Tao*; he is capable of realizing all the virtues of *Tao* (or Heaven and Earth) because he can exhaust or fulfill his own nature or natural inclinations. Tai Chên referred to Mencius' statement that "Form and color are the same as heavenly nature; but only sages can exhaust all that is inherent in form and color" as testifying to the truth of his argument. Man is also capable of bringing harmony and well-being and of preserving life among men because he can comprehend *Tao* and realize the virtues of *Tao*—because he is not separated from Heaven and Earth in his potential nature.

At this point, I should like to make two observations concerning Tai Chên's view of the relation between man and Heaven. First, as has been noted, Tai Chên opposed separating the natural inclinations of man from his nature. Man, besides having desires and feelings, has intelligence and the capacity to know things. But intelligence and desires and feelings are all natural inclinations; they all find their same natural source in *Tao*. Thus, each may be regarded as a different manifestation of the powers of *Tao*. In his *Inquiry into Goodness,* Tai Chên strongly emphasizes that mind and intelligence and the perceptive capacities, such as those of sight, hearing, and other bodily organs, are all caused by Heaven; and that they all are comprehended in natural inclinations. All our perceptual and emotional activities, to the extent that they follow their natural bent without trespassing against universal harmony, are the Way of Heaven. There is no reason, therefore, for discriminating against them because there is no basis to make an absolute dichotomy of mind and intelligence, on the one hand, and desires and feelings, on the other, in terms of their source or origin. The Neo-Confucianists very often identified *Tao* with *li* and called it *t'ien-li* (the heavenly principle or reason) and contrasted this with *ch'i-chih* (the natural or vital endowment). Since there is no metaphysical basis for distinguishing *t'ien-li* from *ch'i-chih*, as both are related to *Tao*, there should be no more disparaging of the natural functions of desires and feelings in man. What really should concern man is how to fulfill his desires without trespassing against the mean and the balance in the universal creative activities of *Tao*.

In pointing out that nature is not separated from natural inclinations and that human nature is not separated from human inclinations, Tai Chên recognized that the inclinations of man differ from those of things in having the special natural inclination toward the principles of reason and righteousness *(li-yi)*, just as the ears have a special natural inclination toward pleasant sounds, and the eyes, toward luxuriant colors. That human beings have mind and intelligence in their natural inclinations differentiates man from things. That the mind and intelligence of man have a natural inclination toward the principles of reason and righteousness indicates man's capacity for developing into sagehood, because mind and intelligence are faculties that enable man to comprehend principles or reason and righteousness, to see what is appropriate for action in a situation. They are therefore most subtle and sensitive. When they are fully developed, they are capable of moral deliberation that makes man free and participating in the activities of *Tao*. In fact, both mind and intelligence and their natural inclinations toward the principles of reason and righteousness are natural endowments of man. This is the reason why man can be said to be naturally good. Goodness in human nature is not something abstract but is formed from these natural endowments of man.

In the light of the natural goodness of human nature, as explained by Tai Chên, not only should it be only natural for man to be moral or virtuous but also moral and ethical and therefore necessary that the development of human nature follow the natural inclination toward the principles of reason and righteousness. Since what is necessary is always congenial with the regularity of *Tao* (Heaven and Earth), it is always natural. In this sense, the Confucian morality and ethics have a naturalistic basis; there is no conflict between the "is" and the "ought" simply because universal nature *(Tao)* contains the moral virtues as a natural component and because that "ought" is a form of being. It is in terms of such a dialectical and dynamic continuum of the moral and the natural that Tai Chên defined the supreme goodness of the nature of Heaven and Earth and the nature of man. Herein also lies the fundamental philosophical reason why Tai Chên advocated the thought of Mencius but strongly opposed that of Kao Tzǔ and Hsün Tzǔ, who had both anticipated, according to Tai Chên, certain undesirable doctrines of the Neo-Confucianists.

It must be noted, however, that, although mind and intelligence are naturally good, they may become beclouded when they are not developed properly. To develop them properly is to concentrate on learning. Tai Chên's explanation of learning *(hsüeh)* is somewhat cursory. He merely suggested that learning consists in "understanding goodness."[41] But the problem is how to "understand goodness." Since goodness consists in benevolence, propriety, and righteousness, to genuinely understand goodness is to comprehend and practice benevolence, propriety, and righteousness. It is the same as seeing what is universal in human desires and feelings, discerning what is the appropriate action in a human situation or relationship, and developing all virtues. It is also essentially the same as expanding and cultivating what is already inherent in the mind and intelligence by checking against the resulting comprehension of the mind. Tai Chên believed that when mind and intelligence achieve understanding in this sense, they will become enlightened; i.e., they will become conscious, and in complete control, of themselves and do everything right on right occasions. In this way, the totality of human nature will be fulfilled, at which stage mind and intelligence are completed or perfected in the sagely wisdom *(shêng-chih)* that is inexhaustible in its use and is consistent with the activities of Heaven and Earth.

In the *Inquiry into Goodness,* Tai Chên suggests that mind and intelligence have great potentiality and that their function, when fulfilled, will lead man to supreme goodness. The important point to be observed is that the attainment of supreme goodness or heavenly virtue cannot be easily conceived of in terms of the mere intellectual understanding of mind and intelligence. It is rather the intellectual understanding of mind and intelligence that leads to the realization and exhibition of virtues to which Tai Chên referred as "supreme illumination" *(shên-ming)*. That *Tao* or Heaven and Earth has these virtues, I have already shown. But because *Tao* or Heaven and Earth also possesses virtue-comprehending human faculties, such as mind and intelligence, in their creative and ordering functionings, Tai Chên described the functions and the virtues of mind and intelligence as being continuous and corresponding with those of *Tao* or Heaven and Earth.[42]

THE METAPHYSICAL FOUNDATION OF MORAL VIRTUES

We now come to the question regarding the metaphysical foundation of moral virtues such as benevolence, propriety, and righteousness;[43] and the ethical relationships such as those between ruler and minister, father and son, wife and husband, older brother and younger brother, and friend and friend. The creative activity of *Tao* is said by Tai Chên to be a virtue of benevolence. But since the creative activity of *Tao* is also an ordering activity, the ordering of things by *Tao* also reveals the fundamental virtues of *Tao*. Thus, Tai Chên said that the very order of things produced by the ordering activity of *Tao* is a virtue of propriety; and that the very distinction drawn by *Tao* in its ordering activity is ultimately a virtue of righteousness. In this metaphysical use, benevolence, propriety, and righteousness are taken to be metaphysical characteristics of *Tao*; and they denote respectively those natural qualities of being creative, order-giving, and individuative of *Tao*.

The reason why Tai Chên used ethical terms to describe the activities of *Tao* is that he believed that it is within the function and structure of a universal principle that man acts and things operate. Tai Chên's argument may be explained as follows: If man participates in *Tao* and is not separated from it, the realization of ethical virtues certainly can be regarded as the realization of the virtues of *Tao*; therefore, by implication, the ethical virtues belong to the true nature of *Tao*. In fact, it is already asserted by Confucius and other Classical Confucianists[44] that only man can realize, make explicit, and expand *Tao*. Tai Chên elaborated this doctrine by formulating the regularity of Heaven and Earth in terms of the three metaphysical virtues. According to Tai Chên, the three metaphysical virtues constitute the basis of the goodness of *Tao* of Heaven and Earth[45]—metaphysical virtues that are not separated from the ethical virtues, just as Heaven and Earth are not separated from man. In man are seen the activities and potential of Heaven and Earth; in ethical virtues, the true virtues and powers of Heaven and Earth. At the same time, the metaphysical virtues of Heaven and Earth are the basis of human value and virtue; hence, man should realize and conform to human nature through realizing, and conforming to, the metaphysical virtues of Heaven and Earth.

The ethical and metaphysical, like the *ming* and *hsing,* are two manners of describing the actual and the ideal —the factual and the potential—aspects of man and Heaven. Here, Tai Chên's distinction between what is natural and what is necessary in a man becomes relevant. All the higher capacities in man, such as mind and intelligence and his capacities for performing virtues, are what are naturally inherent in man. Further, it is natural that man should have his individual human qualities. But whether man fulfills his capacities to the utmost is a matter of individual development and cultivation. If man is to conform to the metaphysical virtues of *Tao,* it is necessary that he develop his nature and capacities to the utmost; and if man develops his nature and capacities without omission, he is said to realize the virtue of Heaven and Earth, which is also the virtue of man. Tai Chên called this virtue of man—a result of the development of human nature in conformity with the activities of Heaven and Earth—*li* or principle. In this sense, *li* is again not an abstraction, a principle to be grasped, as was the case in the Neo-Confucian practice of eliminating one's desires.

That the metaphysical attributes of *Tao,* in terms of benevolence, propriety, and righteousness, give rise to and correspond to the moral virtues—of benevolence, propriety, and righteousness—in Tai Chên's philosophy of goodness, can also be shown. *Tao* or Heaven and Earth as characterized by their creative, individualizing, and harmonizing functions is goodness: goodness that is seen in terms of the metaphysical virtues of benevolence, propriety, and righteousness; and goodness that is displayed in the derivation of human nature from *Tao* or Heaven and Earth. As human nature is not separated from *Tao* in its potentiality, human nature can comprehend and realize the metaphysical attributes of *Tao* in terms of the moral virtues in the context of human fellowship. Mind and intelligence are the capacities for comprehending these virtues. Moreover, as mind itself contains the very virtue of benevolence, it is extremely sensitive, empathically energetic, and highly creative; thus, when mind is rightly exposed, it will develop what is inherent in it and thus regulate every desire and feeling and act of man from its natural state of tranquility to its natural state of harmony. All desires of bodily organs are *jên* when fulfilled in accordance with the regulations of mind and are therefore creative and beneficial. The ultimate goal of man is to attain the supreme goodness that is described in terms of the three virtues of benevolence, propriety, and righteousness. To attain this is to understand the virtues and to practice them.

The question arises how the three virtues of benevolence, propriety, and righteousness can actually be understood and practiced by man. To answer this, Tai Chên introduced the Confucian virtues as being the consequence of the effort to understand and practice the metaphysical virtues or the goodness of *Tao*. He pointed out that one may approximate benevolence by understanding and practicing the faithfulness or truthfulness to oneself *(chung)*; that one may approximate propriety by understanding and practicing integrity or truthfulness to others *(hsin)*; that one may approximate righteousness by understanding and practicing empathy and compassion *(shu)*. He further defined these approximate virtues: to fulfill one's capabilities is truthfulness to oneself; to fulfill one's understanding is truthfulness to others; to be fair in one's giving is compassion.[46]

Tai Chên emphasized that it is through the most intimate experience of man's desires and feelings, by doing what is proper and appropriate in each different situation of life, and by following what is upright and orderly that man will approximate benevolence, propriety, and righteousness; and that a man truthful to himself and others will be unselfish, sincere, and straightforward. When all these virtues are fulfilled, man will possess the virtue of wisdom *(chih)*, because only then will he truly comprehend the goodness in *Tao* and the virtue of courage *(yung)*, as a result of his serious and consistent practice of virtues to attain the supreme good. A man who develops these virtues and concentrates on the performance of these virtues is called a "superior man" *(chün-tzŭ)*; a man who is able to develop and accomplish these virtues from his nature is called a "sage" *(shêng)*. In this way, what is natural in man is finally completed in what is necessary and essential in *Tao*. The ethical virtues of man obtain not only a sanction but also a confirmation in the metaphysical nature of *Tao* or Heaven and Earth. The metaphysical theory of *Tao,* as discussed here, can then be said to provide a sanction and justification for moral virtues, whereas moral virtues provide a confirmation for the metaphysical nature of man. The ethical theory in Confucian philosophy is always embedded in, and consistent with, a theory of reality and a theory of human nature, and this is nowhere as evident, as explicit, and as clear as we find in Tai Chên's concept of goodness.

To emphasize, I repeat that Tai Chên regarded goodness and nature as being interpenetrated, although nature refers to concrete things and developments and goodness, to the balanced and perfect development of natural things. When a thing is called good, that thing must be in accord with the nature of Heaven and Earth. Different things may have different natures, but their goodness is always one. In the light of these explanations, the significance of Tai Chên's assertion in the following should stand out immediately:

> What is necessary is goodness; what is natural is nature. To develop into what is necessary is just to complete and perfect what is natural. This is called the utmost of the natural. It is in terms of this that the Way of Heaven, Earth, Man and everything else be fulfilled.[47]

The total ethical order among men *(jên-lun)* is also a fulfillment of the natural in man; it therefore has a basis in the nature of *Tao*; and it can be described in terms of the five human relationships, referred to as the Way of Man *(jên-tao)* in the *Chung Yung* [Doctrine of the Mean], because man cannot act outside the context of these relationships. These five human relationships, on the one hand, owe their existence to the nature of man and the nature of *Tao*; on the other hand, they must prescribe how human beings should act and live in the context of these relationships. It is in terms of these prescriptions that the nature of man is defined; and it is by following these prescriptions that the nature of man will be developed. According to Mencius, these prescriptions are as follows: between father and son, there must be affection *(ch'in)*; between ruler and subject, there must be righteousness *(yi)*; between husband and wife, there must be discrimination *(pieh)*; between the elder and younger brothers, there must be orderliness *(hsü)*; between friend and friend, there must be truthfulness *(hsin)*. Affection, righteousness, distinction, orderliness, and truthfulness are all the virtues that man is capable of attaining. They are natural to him. But that he should develop and cherish these virtues is a moral requirement and necessity that is rooted in the nature of man and in the nature of *Tao*. These notions of virtues and their sanction may be put succinctly as: "If you can, then you must, but what you must, you can too." Both moral obligation and moral capacities are rooted in the nature of man, which is an extension of the nature of Heaven and Earth.

I have attempted to show above how Tai Chên formulated Classical Confucian ethics in terms of his doctrine of nature, which is natural; and goodness, which is the necessary or the obligatory. It is a doctrine that synthesizes deontology and naturalism through an ontology of man and *Tao* and their dialectical relationship. All the precepts that should govern the basic five human relationships are the basis for the cardinal virtues—benevolence, propriety, and righteousness—which we have described and which represent the development and fulfillment of human nature and the nature of *Tao* in perfect and balanced form.

What I wish to point out further is that Tai Chên, consistent with his reconstruction of Classical Confucianism, held that not only do virtues have a natural basis in man but they also are part of the daily human relationships; for it is in the context of daily life and human relationships that man discovers virtues such as benevolence, propriety, and righteousness. Since any given basic human relationship presupposes, and gives rise to, all other human relationships, it can be shown that each of the basic virtues also presupposes, and gives rise to, other virtues. There is another reason for the interrelation of virtues: All virtues are nothing but the Way of Man in his creative activity. They vary according to different situations and relationships. Essentially, they all pertain to the preservation of human society and the development of individual natures in a social context. That is why benevolence, as the virtue of preserving life among men and of developing individual natures in the context of man, is considered the most basic virtue. Every imperfection regarding the practice of other virtues can be traced to an imperfection in the practice of benevolence. Propriety and righteousness are the most conspicuous and concrete results of practicing benevolence, as we have seen earlier in connection with the three vital functions of *Tao.* They are all based on the patterning and ordering activities of *Tao,* just as benevolence is based on the creative activity of *Tao.* Since the patterning and ordering activities of *Tao* are at the same time the creative activity of *Tao,* a man of true benevolence is at the same time a man of propriety and righteousness. Tai Chên thus saw an organic interrelationship among all the fundamental virtues in the *Analects* of Confucius.

There remain two other virtues, sincerity *(ch'êng)* and moral deliberation *(ch'üan),* which, though not appearing prominently in the *Analects,* received special consideration by Tai Chên. Sincerity is explained by him as what is real *(shih)* and truthful. It is the same as goodness. It is the completion of the development of virtues such as *jên, chih,* and *yung* in conformity with benevolence, propriety, and righteousness. Hence, it is rooted in the reality of daily life and human relationships and starts with the vital intelligent activities of individual men; it then leads to the reality of moral enlightenment of *chih, jên,* and *yung.* But it may also start with learning and moral enlightenment and then proceed to a state of perfection in daily life. The former is referred to in the *Doctrine of the Mean* as a process that starts with sincerity and moves on to enlightenment; the latter, as a process that starts with enlightenment and moves on to sincerity.

The virtue of moral deliberation is the ability of a person to weigh values given in a human situation and to make right decisions for action and self-cultivation. Every human situation and relationship must have its regularity or a principle that is its internal patterning and ordering. *Ch'üan* is the ability to discern the regularity of principle therein and is therefore essential to the development of the human virtues. But a human situation may vary according to different occasions. What is most valuable on one occasion may become the least valuable on another. *Ch'üan* is the ability of a man to discern the change in a situation; it is thus the intrinsic appropriateness of an action. Thus *ch'üan* is in effect the utmost development of wisdom *(chih)* or the understanding of things. But the utmost development of *chih* does not involve abolishment of desires and feelings; it rather depends upon the satisfaction of feelings and desires of all men, leading to the right placing of things in the right places and to the understanding of proper values of feelings and desires. To have this understanding is to have *ch'üan*.

Since the Neo-Confucianists did not recognize the proper value and significance of a moral life in terms of a universal comprehension of feelings and a universal satisfaction of vital desires, they lacked the understanding of the virtue of *ch'üan*. Because of this, Tai Chên implicitly suggested that their minds, in a sense, were beclouded. I shall discuss this point in the following section.

PROBLEMS OF REMOVING SELFISHNESS AND BECLOUDEDNESS

In explaining *Tao* and individual things in terms of goodness, Tai Chên inevitably left unresolved the problem of evil and wrongdoing. If man has intrinsic goodness in his nature and is naturally capable of cultivating himself into a sage, then the question arises how the presence of evil and wrongdoing in life should be accounted for. That man has notions of evil and wrongdoing is empirically obvious. It is further true that, in general, man can make a distinction between what ought to be desired and what ought not to be desired. We are aware that performing what ought to be desired in a situation may entail personal unhappiness and that performing what ought not to be desired may sometimes entail personal happiness. But we usually consider our acts as being wrong if we perform what we ought not to do merely on the basis of avoiding personal unhappiness or pursuing personal happiness. We need an explanation and a justification of what we would in general call evil and wrongdoing. The question is whether this justification and this explanation are possible and intelligible in Tai Chên's philosophy of goodness.

It is important to point out that notions of evil and wrongdoing in Chinese philosophy, in an important sense, are different from the notion of evil in Christianity and in some post-Christian Western philosophies. When Christians declare that there is original sin in man because the first man disobeyed God and, therefore, that man needs God's grace and love for salvation, it is implied that man's soul contains some positive evil even before he was born. This evil can be simply defined as sinfulness against the will of God: What is evil or wrong is always what God forbids. To commit the act that God forbids is also evil. What is good and right is what God approves of or demands. To do or to desire what is good or right is good and right. It is in terms of the will of God that good and bad, right and wrong, are defined, explained, and justified.

In contrast to this theological explanation and justification of good and evil are the moral notions of goodness and evilness in the Confucian philosophy,[48] in which the term "evil" *(o)* or "not-good" *(pu-shan)* is always used in a moral sense. Something is evil or wrong or not good, not because the will of God is disobeyed, but because human nature is disobeyed and because it leads to undesirable consequences. Indeed, it is a distinguishing mark of Chinese philosophy in general and of Confucian philosophy in particular that morality has never been based upon a notion of a supernatural and personal God. Morality is a matter of humanity. It is perfectly defined, explained, and justified within the nature of *Tao* and thus within the nature of man. And because morality is justified, explained, and defined within the nature of man, it has a natural basis— not a supernatural basis—and thus becomes autonomous. As explained earlier, Classical Confucianism implicitly prescribes that to be moral is to cultivate the natural but refined part of man, which is the goodness inherent in man. But autonomy of morality does not preclude its having an ultimate source and justification in the metaphysics and cosmology of *Tao*, as the nature of man is always continuous, and consistent with, the nature of *Tao*, in which is found the matrix of goodness.

In the light of such a philosophy, goodness and righteousness are positive values, whereas evil or wrongdoing are negative values. Evil and wrongdoing denote only the lack of goodness or righteousness.[49] Thus Confucius and Mencius rarely spoke of evil or wrongdoing as such but only of the lack of benevolence *(pu-jên)*, the lack of faithfulness *(pu-hsin)*, the lack of righteousness *(pu-yi)*, and the like. This means that the specific evil or wrongdoing is due to the lack of self-cultivation or the loss of the basic goodness in human nature brought on by the influence of specific circumstances.[50] Evil or wrongdoing is never taken to be inherent in man or as previously existing in *Tao*. Mencius specifically talked about the original goodness of man, as man can immediately experience goodness under certain actual conditions. Confucius spoke of the nature of men being similar in their capacities for achieving goodness *(jên)*, even though their minds can be either dull or intelligent. Dullness is neither evil nor wrongdoing; and the capacity to achieve *jên* is certainly goodness. Finally, in the *Doctrine of the Mean* and the *Book of Changes,* it is explicitly asserted that human nature is derived from the nature of *Tao*, which is absolutely and supremely good.

I have pointed out earlier that, although writing in the Confucian tradition, Hsün Tzǔ affirmed the evil nature of man: that the evil that is ascribed to human nature is brought on by the fact that man can expand his desires for profit, comfort, and sensual pleasures. Evil here is affirmed as a form of undesirable social experience that results from a lack of restraint and control. That a man can exert control and restraint (temperance), however, is affirmed in Hsün Tzǔ's philosophy. Accordingly, despite human nature that tends toward evil because of the presence of desires, human mind and intelligence are the instruments of *Tao* and are thus capable of regulating human nature into goodness by having the rules of propriety established. In the light of this explanation, it is evident that, even in the case of Hsün Tzǔ, evil or wrongdoing is possible, not because of the intrinsic qualities in man, but because of the unrestrained expansion of the self-interest and desires in man. Evil can be completely avoided or eliminated by the conscientious efforts of human reason, thus ensuring the autonomy of morality.[51]

As has been noted, the Neo-Confucianists were the first to attribute evil or wrongdoing to the inherent and natural qualities of man. Their distinction between *ch'i-chih* and *yi-li*—or between mind and conscience, on the one hand, and the desires and feelings, on the other—allows them to think of evil or wrongdoing as part of human nature and to consequently condemn human desires and feelings as completely devoid of *li* or goodness. Indeed, the Neo-Confucianists might have accepted the idea that man can achieve complete goodness in a physical life; but, even if they had, their distinction between the good and the evil in human nature should not have permitted a complete removal of evil in human nature because human nature does embody natural qualities such as feelings and desires— feelings and desires, which the Neo-Confucianists thought were devoid of goodness.

I have shown how Tai Chên argued against this Neo-Confucian theory of the metaphysical bifurcation between nature and natural inclinations and the theory of evilness of natural inclinations. It needs no elaboration to show that Tai Chên's philosophy of goodness, to the extent that I have explained it, fortified his criticism of the Neo-Confucian ideas and buttressed his claim to have revealed the true basis of Confucian philosophy. For Tai Chên, evil or wrongdoing is not inherent or original in human nature, since human nature is a continuum of intelligence, feelings, and desires, all derived from, and also manifesting, the nature of *Tao*. Thus any evil or wrongdoing must be due to contingencies in the empirical developments of human capacities. In fact, according to Tai Chên, evil or wrongdoing is considered as the specific failure of individual men in achieving such virtues as benevolence, propriety, and righteousness.

In the *Inquiry into Goodness,* Tai Chên shows that evil or wrongdoing, as found in specific cases, is due to the lack of fulfillment of the natural inclinations of man; therefore, that special evil or wrongdoing stems from individual imperfection. As shown earlier, Tai Chên argued that the development and perfection of human nature consist in satisfying and respecting desires and feelings of men without inappropriateness and disharmony. Thus, it was only natural for Tai Chên to hold that, in the final analysis, evil or wrongdoing results from the satisfaction of one's own desires and the respecting of one's own feelings without satisfying the desires (or perhaps without hindering the satisfaction of the desires of other men) and respecting the feelings of other men. Evil can be further identified with the failure of mind and intelligence to attain a comprehension of virtue and to secure guidance in reason for one's desires and feelings.

Tai Chên called selfishness *(ssŭ)* the failure to have a universal regard for other men's desires in one's attempt to satisfy his own desires. He also described it as "doing harm to *jên*," which is the creative harmony of things in the world. Likewise, Tai Chên referred to the failure to have universal regard for the feelings of other men in judging other men as partiality (*p'ien*); and, in the light of this understanding, the failure to recognize the true nature of man and the patterning of things and the failure to guide the development of one's nature toward virtue and perfection as beclouding *(pi)*. The problem with the development of a man's nature is not that he has feelings and desires, but that his desires are selfish, his feelings unsympathetic, and his mind and intelligence, beclouded. As Tai Chên saw it, all desires and feelings are intrinsically good because they are not separated from *Tao* or Heaven or Earth. But in order to realize their intrinsic goodness in actual behavior, desires and feelings must be free from selfishness and partiality, and mind and intelligence must be cleansed of becloudings. Hence, Tai Chên said, "If not selfish, then the desires [of a man] are all benevolent, proper, and righteous; if not beclouded, then the intelligence [of a man] is the so-called clarity and sagely wisdom."[52] Tai Chên clearly assumed that man, in the process of developing his nature, may be subject to any of these failures; he may, therefore, incur all specific evils or wrongdoings in personal behavior, in social relationships, and in government.

Now the questions may be raised how selfishness, partiality, and beclouding can be removed and how goodness can be achieved in one's nature. The answers are clearly given in the *Inquiry into Goodness*: to remove selfishness and therefore partiality, there is no better method than to strengthen one's virtue of compassion *(shu)*, which is the universal regard for the desires and feelings of other men. To remove beclouding from one's mind and intelligence, there is no better method than to concentrate on learning *(hsüeh)*. The most important factor for self-improvement in all these, however, should be a recognition of one's selfishness, partiality, and beclouding—and the consequent discontent that results. Once a man is always on the alert for the evil and wrongdoing in his dealings with men, with the management of things, and with the comportment of himself, he would prevent himself from deviating into the track of wrongdoing; and he would feel the urge to develop his nature into the virtues of goodness, benevolence, propriety, and righteousness. This suggests that a man can either avoid or eliminate evilness and wrongfulness if he sets his mind toward the prescribed virtues and practices them constantly. This further suggests that he should follow the good impulses in his nature by becoming aware of the supreme goodness in his nature and in Heaven and Earth as a goal of his conscientious efforts toward perfection. Tai Chên, in the third part of his *Inquiry into Goodness,* gives ample illustration and explanation of what he means by following the virtues of benevolence, propriety, and righteousness as a means of avoiding and eliminating evil and wrongdoing. He is typically Confucian in believing that all specific evil and wrongdoing can be removed and that every man can then become a sage.

Tai Chên, however, gave little attention to how learning *(hsüeh)* is to be used as a method to counter the beclouding in one's mind and intelligence. Objecting to the Neo-Confucian belief that there will be no beclouding if man simply exterminates all of his desires, Tai Chên proposed *hsüeh,* as used in the Classical Confucian sense,[53] as a means to the removal of beclouding. *Hsüeh* involves wide learning, close inquiry, deliberate thinking, and clear discernment; *hsüeh* is for the purpose of practice and doing. In short, *hsüeh* is the inquiry into, and the practice of, virtues by observing the principles and patternings of things; i.e., by seeing reason in the nature of things. In the light of Tai Chên's critique of the Neo-Confucian notion of *li* and in the light of the Neo-Confucian method of investigating *li,* it may perhaps be suggested that beclouding of one's mind and intelligence is reflected in the subjective opinions, which the Neo-Confucianists called "principle" *(li)*; hence, that beclouding leads one to abstract speculation. Thus, to remove beclouding by *hsüeh* is to remove one's private opinions by opening one's mind to actualities and forming accurate notions of them.

What Tai Chên understood by *hsüeh* may even be shown in the light of his own practice of academic inquiry and in his methodology for pursuing the truth. According to Tuan Yü-ts'ai, Tai Chên, as a great master of textual criticism and clear thinking, once remarked:

> We should always understand what Mencius means by specific patterning and ordering. We should obtain the specific patterning and ordering of things. Then, from synthesis to analysis *(fên)* or from analysis to synthesis *(ho)*, there is nothing which cannot be done.[54]

Hsüeh then can be said to consist in finding the specific patterning and ordering of things by the "synthesis" and "analysis" of specific objects. This is directly opposed to the speculative methods of Neo-Confucianism. In applying his method of investigation to the study of the Classical Confucian doctrine, Tai Chên naturally found it necessary to look into the meanings of words as well as institutional histories to discover and understand the truth of *Tao*.

It might be said that Tai Chên oriented his studies in phonological and historical research in his search of the truth of *Tao*. He wrote to Tuan Yü-ts'ai:

> Since I was seventeen years old, I have had the desire to learn *Tao* and told myself that *Tao* can be found only in the Six Classics and the works of Confucius and Mencius. [But if we are to achieve this purpose,] unless we are clear about the meanings of the words, and the institutional background and history, we will not even understand the language of these Classical works.[55]

On another occasion, he said:

> The final goal of the classical learning is [the attainment of the understanding of] *Tao*. To clarify *Tao*, we need words *(tzŭ)*. But words are formed on the basis of the study of meaning and language. From the study of language, we may then understand the true meaning of words [used in the past]. From the understanding of the true meaning of words [in the Classics], we may then comprehend the mind and will of the ancient sages.[56]

Indeed, it may be safely supposed that one of Tai Chên's motivations for his critique of Neo-Confucianism was his belief that the Confucian scholars of the Sung period had not really understood the language and meanings of the words of the ancient sages but only claimed to have understood them by projecting their own opinions into the doctrines of the sages;[57] that this was why the misled Neo-Confucianists themselves were further misleading others. This was also the reason why Tai Chên thought so highly of his *Commentaries on the Meanings of Terms in the* Book of Mencius, in which he applied his method of "synthesis" and "analysis." This attempt at discovering and restoring the true ideas of Confucian teachings is no less manifested in his *Inquiry into Goodness,* which at the same time reveals his original and constructive philosophical ingenuity.

Facsimile of a hand-written letter by Tai Chên (1723–1777), enunciating his methodology and his philosophical attitude. The original is deposited in the National Central Library in Taipei, Taiwan.

一部天圖兩張音均表原底一本想春夏之交乃
得到割圜記考工記圖皆未有其九章算經俟今
人抄出並俟後寄順候
迳祉不宣上

若膺賢弟足下

友生戴震頓首 正月十四

工記圖屈原賦注巳年江南興撫曾取以進館中依例
去之今大著亦不得抄入前歲十月寄謝姓信閏十月
又一信皆收到有寫本音均表兩部此兩信內言七
月寄吳廷芳銀信其人與信皆未見及問之投捐
者云仍令發川省寄上舞春作札詳論韻事寄
龔八公處并寄聲韻考一本此信竟浮沉今將存
稿者附寄餘所言不復記憶笑比時以大著未刻
有所商處今既刻成應撰序嶺兼寄上又上年冬
舍姪朝恩赴川省守備任寄水經注一部經典釋文

深者有歉之後者自謂歉而不明者有幾問其人曰聖

矣乎必不敢任而譏其失理必怒恝是盡人不知已歉

世昔人異於今人一啟口而曰理似今人勝昔人吾謂昔人

之勝今人正在此益昔人所之為於意見今人以不出於私

即謂之理由是以意見殺人咸自信為理矣聊舉一字

言之關乎德行行事匪小僕自上年三月初獲足疾至

今不能出戶又目力大損今夏纂修事似可畢定於七八

月間乞假南旋就醫覰一書院糊口不復出矣竭數年

之力勒成一書明孔孟之道餘力整其從前所訂於字

學經義學者四庫全書例于現在人撰述不錄僕之考

僅、為邪正之別其言存理也又僅、為敬肆之別
不知必敬必正而理猶未得其言人欲所蔽僅、以為
無欲則無蔽不知欲也者相生養之道也餙視人猶己
則忠以已推之則惻憂樂於人則仁出於正不出於邪
則義恭敬不侮慢則禮無差謬則智曰忠恕曰仁
義禮智豈有他哉在常人為欲在君子皆成懿德
使夫欲而後一於理是古賢人聖人體民之情遂民
之欲皆非也況欲之失為私不為欲自以為得理而所
執之理寔是謬乃蔽而不明聖人而下罕能無欲有蔽之

吾言皆承生於其心害於事害於政夫仁義何以禍
斯民觀近儒之言理吾亦知斯民之受其禍之所終
極矣古人曰理解者即尋其脈理而析之也曰天
理者如莊周言依乎天理即所謂彼節者有間也
子貢問有一言而可以終身行之者子曰其恕乎己
所不欲勿施於人大學絜矩之道不過所惡於上毋
以使下云、曰所不欲曰所惡指人之常情不堪受者
耳以己絜之人則理明孟子對齊王好貨好色曰
與百姓同之非權辭也好貨好色欲也與百姓同之即理
也後儒以理欲相對寔雜老氏無欲之說其視理欲也

新正接到上年八月

手翰并六書音均表三部銀四十兩謀之知仍已有高順政

事餘暇無他嗜好孜孜於古遺經不小學誠感心盛

事也僕自十七歲時有志聞道誰非求之六經孔孟

不得非從事於字義制度名物無由以通其語言宗

儒讖訓詁之學輕語言文字是欲渡江河而棄舟楫

欲登高而無階梯也為之卅餘年灼然知古今治亂

之源在是孟子闢楊墨曰率獸食人人將相食詰

告子曰率天下之人而禍仁義兩稱聖人復起不易

Translator's Notes

The original Chinese text of Tai Chên's *Yüan Shan* [Inquiry into Goodness] that I used as the basis of my English translation is taken from volume 6 of the *An Hui Ts'ung Shu* [Series of Books about An Hui Province], published in 1936 by the An Hui Ts'ung Shu Editing and Printing Office. This anthology includes twelve works by Tai Chên. The *Inquiry into Goodness* is the first of these and occupies a space of twenty-four double-leaf pages. It was apparently reprinted from an earlier version of 1777, which was edited and proofread by Li Wei, of Fukien Province. In this edition, the *Inquiry into Goodness* is separated into three parts *(chüan)* and has a brief preface by Tai Chên explaining his purpose for writing it. The first part has eleven sections; the second, five sections; and the last, sixteen sections. My English translation preserves the ordering of the sections found in the Chinese text. As there is no division between paragraphs in the Chinese text, it needs to be noted that I broke each section into paragraphs where it seems natural to do so. All translations of quoted passages are my own unless indicated otherwise.

In the process of translating the *Inquiry into Goodness*, I have also consulted the following versions: *Yüan Shan: Mêng Tzŭ tzŭ-yi shu-chêng* [Commentary on the Meanings of Terms in the *Book of Mencius*], punctuated and edited by Chang Hsi-shen (Shanghai: Ku Chi Publishing Company, 1956); *Tai Tung-yüan chi* [Collection of Essays of Tai Tung-yüan], edited by Wang Yün-wu (Shanghai: The Commercial Press, 1933) and reprinted in 1965 by the same press in Taipei.

The *Inquiry into Goodness* consists of three parts. The first part concerns Tai Chên's philosophy of the goodness of nature [the Way of Heaven]. Every attribute of ultimate reality and virtues are defined, explained, and justified in terms of goodness. Goodness is seen in benevolence *(jên)*, propriety *(li)*, righteousness *(yi)*, the Way *(tao)*, virtue *(tê)*, nature *(hsing)*, necessity *(ming)*, natural endowments *(ts'ai)*, and further in every action and patterning of things in the world. Goodness is in substance identified with the primary creative activity *(shêng-shêng)* of the Way and the Way's consequent producing of the patterning and ordering *(t'iao-li)* of things. Later quotations from the *Yi Ching* [Book of Changes], the *Li Chi* [Record of Rites], the *Mêng Tzŭ* [Book of Mencius], and the *Chung Yung* [Doctrine of the Mean] suffice to indicate the sources of Tai Chên's own cosmological and metaphysical ideas.

The second part concerns the nature of things and men. Human nature is explained in terms of comparisons with heavenly attributes. It is affirmed that every human physical desire has its natural inclination, which should be respected and preserved, and that the human mind has a special inclination for benevolence that makes possible men's achievement of moral illumination. Later quotations from *Tso Chuan* [Tso's Commentary on the *Spring and Autumn Annals*], the *Book of Mencius,* and the *Record of Rites* supply materials for Tai Chên's discussions on human nature, human mind, human soul, and their relationship to the ultimate Way.

The final part discusses the sources of evil or wrongdoing in terms of the partiality of individual desires and feelings and the beclouding in the individual mind and intelligence. By quoting and explaining passages from the *Lun Yü* [Analects], the *Doctrine of the Mean*, the *Record of Rites,* the *Shih Ching* [Book of Poetry], Tai Chên shows how man may attain goodness by avoiding the selfishness of desires and feelings and the obscuration of mind and intelligence.

Tai Chên's Preface

When I started writing my treatise *Yüan Shan,*[1] in three chapters *(san-chüan)*, I was afraid that scholars might be biased by their own interpretations of my point of view; hence, I quoted from the Confucian Classics[2] to explain and support my argument. In the volume to follow, the main body of my discussion is divided into three chapters; these are followed by my quotations from, and comments on, the Classics. Since I have compared and combined the meanings of terms in the Classics, it should be very clear where the beginning and the end of my reasoning and my purpose lie: an examination of the Way of Heaven *(t'ien-tao)*[3] and the Way of Man;[4] they present the most excellent teachings of the Classics. Now that we are separated from the ancient Sages by such a long period of time, it is no surprise that students of the Classics in our time cannot maintain a systematic view of the teachings or the insights of the ancient Sages and that they accept what they usually hear and learn about without discriminating the true from the false. Fearing that my words are not strong enough to correct this tendency, I therefore hide my treatise in my family library *(chia-shu)*[5] in the hope that some able person will discover it and that he will some day promote the truth contained therein.

Chapter 1

Goodness *(shan)*[1] consists of benevolence *(jên)*,[2] propriety *(li)*,[3] and righteousness *(yi)*.[4] These three principles are the great norms under Heaven. When the first goodness is exhibited in the Way of Heaven, it is called concordance *(shun)*;[5] when it is substantiated into an illustrious virtue, it is called faith *(hsin)*;[6] when it is followed [by the people] so that they may attain the specific principles of reason, it is called regularity *(ch'ang)*.[7] [When we speak of] the Way of Heaven, we refer to the ceaselessness of the process of the formation and transformation *(hua)* [of goodness];[8] [when we speak of] virtue, we refer to the incorruptibility [of goodness]; when we speak of principles or reason, we refer to the completeness and subtleness of goodness. [When we speak of goodness,] we include, as a whole, man's understanding of regularity, his experience of faith, and his attainment of concordance. When we speak of nature *(hsing)*,[9] we refer to what accords with the process of the formation and transformation of Heaven and Earth,[10] by which various kinds of things are formed and differentiated from one another. That a thing is confined to what it obtains from the process of the formation and transformation of Heaven and Earth is called necessity *(ming)*;[11] that a thing is produced in accordance with a pattern of design is called nature. That a thing takes shape and acquires its attributes according to its nature, with some excellence *(hsiu)*,[12] emanating from its inner being and manifested in or through appearance, color, and sound is called ability *(ts'ai)*.[13] It is things, or matters of fact, that are nurtured [and indeed developed] by nature; it is capability *(nêng)*[14] that enforces control and temperance within a thing itself. Matters of fact and capability are differentiated from one another, and this is due to the ability that is inherent in things. Ability, in turn, is subject to classification, owing to [the power of nature].

Because there are blood and breath *(hsüeh-ch'i)*, intelligence and mind *(hsin-chih)*[15] exist, as do things and the capabilities inherent in things. Because there are mind and intelligence, the superior man knows that the perfection of the Way of Man depends completely upon nature. When he looks at the signs of the natural *(chêng)*, [16]he knows the beginning of things; when he cherishes the virtue of supreme illumination *(shên-ming)*,[17] he knows the end of things. Proceeding from mind and intelligence to the attainment of the virtue of supreme intelligence, [the superior man] in his treatment of things in the world will cause the world to return to [the principles of] benevolence; and in his treatment of the capability inherent in things, he will cause the world to follow wisdom *(chih)*.[18]

By reason of its incorruptibility, we call goodness faith; by reason of its unity and diversity, we call it the norm for flexible evaluation *(ch'üan)*.[19] By reason of the harmony of Heaven and Earth resulting from goodness, we realize that goodness is the Way *(tao)*.[20] By reason of the faith based on goodness, we realize that goodness is virtue *(tê)*.[21] On the one hand, the Way is what prevails in human relationships and among common things; on the other hand, what is equal to the productive power of Heaven and Earth is called sincerity *(ch'êng)*,[22] and what obeys the control of nature is called necessity. Hence, we may say that the creative activity of Heaven and Earth is the origin of the process of the formation and transformation of things; and that the creative activity of Heaven and Earth in accordance with the principles of order and reason *(t'iao-li)*[23] is characteristic of the flow of such a formation and transformation *(hua)*.[24]

What is most comprehensive under heaven is the productive movement [of Heaven and Earth]; what is most simple under heaven is the seclusive quietude of Heaven and Earth *(t'ien-ti)*.[25] The comprehensiveness of productive movement is characteristic of the life of Heaven and Earth, and the simplicity of quietude is characteristic of their quiescence. What has life is [always in] movement and [is incessantly] productive; what is at rest is always tranquil and self-rectifying.

When the superior man conducts inquiries for the sake of increasing his learning, he follows the principle of active production as exhibited in the life of Heaven and Earth; when he manages to meet the mind of Heaven and Earth in pure unison, he follows the principle of simplicity as exhibited in the quiescence of Heaven and Earth. The activation of human nature is comparable to the life of Heaven and Earth, and the existence of human nature is comparable to the quiescence of Heaven and Earth. Only when there is life is there rest; and only when there is quiescence is there life.[26] [This explains how and why] Heaven and Earth make the formation and transformation of things possible. Hence, we may say that the creative productiveness of Heaven and Earth is benevolence and that this creative productiveness in accordance with the principles of order and reason is propriety and righteousness. What then is propriety? Its distinguishing mark is found in the ordering of things after the principles of order and reason. And what is righteousness? Its distinguishing mark is found in the control and order in nature after the principles of order and reason.

One who acquires the creative productiveness of Heaven and Earth is benevolent; one who acquires the principles of order and reason is wise. It must be easy to follow one who has attained the utmost in benevolence; and it must be simple to understand one who has attained the utmost in wisdom. It is from benevolence and wisdom that all moral principles are generated. For this reason, one who acquires the creative productiveness of Heaven and Earth is benevolent; one who acquires the principles of order and reason is proper;[27] one who is resolute in his moral judgments is righteous; and one who does not exhibit his subjectivity is wise. Finally, one who possesses benevolence and wisdom and follows the principles of equilibrium and harmony *(chung-ho)*[28] is called a sage *(shêng-jên)*.[29]

Wisdom will enable men to understand the principles of propriety and righteousness; when these are understood, we shall know how to fulfill the needs of mankind and how to cultivate the virtues of proper human relationships. The most lofty virtue is benevolence. With benevolence, there arises the dual relationship of love and respect between father and son. With propriety, one is able to fulfill one's obligations to friends and relatives, close and distant, superior and inferior, by adhering to the virtues proper to these relationships. With righteousness, one is able to meet the right ends of things and therefore do justice to them. After a man has immersed himself in wisdom, he will be able to cope with Heaven and Earth and with ten thousand things in the world. Finally, when one becomes creatively productive and is capable of regulating things according to the principles of order and reason, he is a sage.

The *Hsi T'zŭ Ta Chuan* [Great Appendixes] in the *Yi Ching* [Book of Changes] says:

> That which transcends form is the Way, and that which exists within material form is determinate.

What exists within form acquires its existence by taking on a form and a substance; what transcends form is the *yin* and the *yang*,[30] and the *kuei* and the *shên*,[31] which form the essence of things. Therefore, it is said in the *Chung Yung* [Doctrine of the Mean]:

> The virtues of the *kuei* and *shên* are great indeed! You look but will not see them, you listen but will not hear them. But they comprehend all things and leave nothing out.[32]

It is said in the *Hung Fan* [Great Norm]:[33]

> There are five activating forces *(wu-hsing)*[34] under heaven: the first one is called water; the second, fire; the third, wood; the fourth, metal; the fifth, soil.

When the five activating forces take on form and substance, they become determinate things. When they become detached from physical form and nature and form the essence of things, the five activating forces constitute the Way. That is to say, the five activating forces, together with *yin* and *yang*, are those things that, when acquired by things in the world, give these things their essential nature.

The *Great Appendixes* of the *Book of Changes* says:

> The successive movement of the *yin* and *yang* constitutes what is called the Way. That which carries on this movement is goodness; that which perfects this movement is its nature.

By the successive movement of the *yin* and *yang* is meant the ceaseless process of the formation and transformation of Heaven and Earth: this is the Way. Is it not true that the successive movement of the *yin* and *yang* is what makes the creative productiveness of Heaven and Earth possible? Is it not also true that this successive movement of *yin* and *yang* is also what causes the creative activity of Heaven and Earth to follow the principles of order and reason? From this, we see how and why Heaven and Earth proceed in concordance. This is the reason why it is said, "the successive movement of *yin* and *yang* constitutes what is called the Way."

The creative productiveness of Heaven and Earth is due to benevolence. There is no presence of the creative productiveness of Heaven and Earth that is not accompanied by the principles of order and reason. The orderliness in the patterns of things in following the principles of order and reason is best manifested in propriety *(li)*;[35] the resoluteness of the human mind in following the principles of order and reason is best manifested in righteousness.[36] On the basis of these—propriety and righteousness—we recognize the regularity of the laws of Heaven and Earth. When a man attains all three [propriety, righteousness, and benevolence], he then possesses the great virtues of mankind under heaven, and we have a paradigm of human behavior. Thus, it is said: "What carries on the movement of *yin* and *yang* is goodness." By this, we mean that in considering the creation of men and things, we recognize that the goodness in their natures uninterruptedly carries on the activity of Heaven and Earth.

Only after there are Heaven and Earth are there men and things. After there are men and things, there are distinctions between the qualities of their endowments from Heaven and Earth. What determines the qualities that a thing possesses is its nature. Both men and things have desires *(yü).*[37] What is called desire is the function of the nature of a thing. Both men and things have perception *(chüeh).*[38] What is referred to as perception is the content of the nature of a thing. We say that to have desires without being selfish is to be benevolent; to have perceptions without being biased is to be wise. When a man acquires benevolence and wisdom, he adds nothing to either the function or the content of his nature; he merely exercises the inherent virtue of his nature. Viewed from the standpoint of the natural, the natures of men and things are called concordance;[39] viewed from the standpoint of necessity, they are called regularity;[40] viewed from the standpoint of their ultimate origin, they are called virtue.[41] The Way under heaven must have its consummation in concordance; all instruction under heaven must take regularity as its norm; all the natures of men and things under heaven are the same in respect to their inherent virtues. The function of natures can be matched with the five activating forces and the *yin* and *yang*; the capability of natures can be matched with the *kuei* and *shên*; the virtue of natures [of men and things] can be matched with that of Heaven and Earth. Although both men and things have desires, the desires they are born with are different;[42] although both men and things have perceptions, their perceptions differ in the brightness and dullness of their capabilities for understanding the great and small things; or for sustaining and reproducing life; or both. The original goodness of both men and things is in agreement with the virtue of Heaven and Earth and consists in the Way. This explains how men and things fulfill their different natures that are derived from the five activating forces and the *yin* and *yang*. Therefore, it is said that "What makes a thing complete and perfect is its nature."

By implication, goodness is the common share[43] of all things and men under heaven; nature is the function and capability by which all men accomplish that goal. Nature is the origin of the acts of men and the movements of things. This so-called goodness is just this. We can recognize the presence of goodness by observing the process of the formation and transformation of Heaven and Earth and the function and capability of the natures of men and things. When the superior man communicates his teachings to other men, he rectifies the behavior of men by reference to the common goal. When the function and capability of men's nature conforms to the common goal, it is judged to be upright and balanced; when it does not so conform, it is considered sinister and perverse. The superior man also teaches the regularity of Heaven and Earth so that people may know that they should follow this regularity. Only when one has been clear about the concordance of Heaven and Earth may another speak with him of the Way; only when one has observed the regularity of Heaven and Earth may another speak with him of goodness; and finally, only when one has penetrated into the virtue of Heaven and Earth may another speak with him of nature.[44]

The *Great Appendixes* of the *Book of Changes* says:

> The great virtue of Heaven and Earth is the giving and preserving of life.

The principle of materialization of vital forces into things of determinate kinds could be summed up in one phrase— the creative productiveness of Heaven and Earth. Once this principle is discerned, one will know benevolence; once one discerns the principles of order and reason, one will know propriety. It could not be that Heaven and Earth could be creatively productive without exhibiting in their products patterns that follow the principles of order and reason.

From this, we may know righteousness.[45] Is it not true that both propriety and righteousness are manifestations of benevolence?[46] A mind that acquires the principles of order and reason and therefore exhibits orderly patterns in its thoughts in accordance with the principles of order and reason can be said to be wise. Is it not hidden in wisdom that one may find benevolence? That Heaven and Earth are full of creative productiveness and produce things in accordance with the principles of order and reason "manifests the virtue of benevolence."[47] It is precisely because there are principles of order and reason in the production of things that Heaven and Earth have their creative productivity: the principles of order and reason are "implicit in the creative activity of Heaven and Earth." It is in the manifest aspects of Heaven and Earth that we perceive the life of Heaven and Earth in their formation and transformation. Life is that which has the greatest movement and which is capable of regulating things in accordance with the principles of order and reason; quiescence is that which has the greatest tranquility and makes use of unpredictable power *(shên)*. From the growing of the trunks, the leaves, the blossoms, and the fruits of trees, we shall observe the life-processes of Heaven and Earth; but it is from the white kernel of a fruit that completes the nature of life that we shall observe the quiescence of Heaven and Earth. Therefore, the capability of creative activity is called benevolence; it is the origin from which everything is begotten *(yüan)*;[48] the capability of regulating things in accordance with the principles of order and reason is called propriety; it is what pushes the nature of a thing forward toward completion *(hêng)*;[49] the capability of investigating the principles of order and reason and of using them as a basis for judgments of matters of fact is called righteousness, which is usefulness *(li)* [which furthers the concordance of Heaven and Earth];[50] finally, the capability of acquiring the right criteria of order and reason[51] and of keeping them in mind as guiding principles of life is called wisdom. Wisdom expresses the correctness and firmness *(chêng)*[52] of the Way of Heaven and Earth and, therefore, their goodness when exhibited in man.

The *Li Chi* [Record of Rites] in its *Yüeh Ch'i* [Record of Music] says:

> All men have blood, breath, mind, and intelligence, but there are no regularities governing their emotions of sorrow, joy, gladness, and anger. All men respond and act according to the external objects that affect them, and from this result the various capacities of the mind.[53]

All those who have blood, breath, mind, and intelligence therefore have desires.

To the extent that the nature of man is evidenced in his desires, there is discrimination between the love and fear of sound, color, smell, and taste; as soon as there are desires, there are feelings. To the extent that the nature of man is evidenced in his feelings, there is discrimination between the balance and imbalance of gladness, anger, sorrow, and joy. As soon as there are desires and feelings, there are skills *(ch'iao)*[54] and wisdom. To the extent that nature is evidenced in skills and wisdom, there is discrimination between the approval and disapproval of good and evil and of right and wrong. The way of sustaining and maintaining life finds its key in desires; the way of sympathy and deep understanding finds its key in feelings. This is because desires and feelings are the signs of the natural.[55] When these two are well regulated, a man is able to preserve and promote the orders of things under heaven. To grasp the essence of what is good and evil, one must use skills, for it is from skills that the rulers and ministers obtain the power of government; to grasp the essence of what is right and what is wrong, one must use wisdom, for it is from wisdom that one acquires the virtue of sagehood. These two, skills and wisdom, are also the signs of nature. If man can master them so thoroughly that they become a necessary part of himself, he will be able to preserve and promote all capabilities of things under heaven.

The *Record of Music* of the *Record of Rites* also says:

That the nature of man is quiescent at his birth is due
to the nature of Heaven. He responds to and acts according
to the external things that affect him, owing to the desires
in his nature. Things come to him more and more, and he
accumulates knowledge. Then his likes and dislikes are
gradually formed. If these are not modulated by anything
within and if he is incapable of coming back to himself in
the face of temptations from without, his heavenly principle
will be extinguished.[56]

Man inherits only his human nature from Heaven; but this
is first called "the nature of blood, breath, mind, and intelligence" and then called "the nature of Heaven"?[57] The
reason is that man derives his physical nature and mental
intelligence from the five activating forces and from *yin*
and *yang*. When the physical and mental intelligence is not
moved by external things and has therefore retained its
purity, it is then called "the nature of Heaven." But this
does not make it essentially different from "blood, breath,
mind, and intelligence." Thus, we may say that the blood
and breath are what form the material of the formation and
transformation of Heaven and Earth; that mind and intelligence are what form the spiritual agency of Heaven and
Earth; that nature is the concordance of Heaven and Earth;
and, finally, that necessity is the regularity of the Way of
Heaven and Earth.

Mencius says:

He who has fulfilled his mental capabilities to the utmost
knows his nature. Knowing his nature, he knows Heaven
(*Book of Mencius,* 7A.1).

The ears, the eyes, and all the other bodily organs desire
those things on which our physical nature depends for
nourishment. The so-called desires of human nature originate from the process of the formation and transformation of
Heaven and Earth. Therefore, in the case of Heaven, they
form the Way of Heaven; in the case of man, they are rooted
in human nature and find expression in his daily affairs; in
this sense, they form the Way of Man. By the same token,

a benevolent and righteous heart also originates from the virtues of Heaven and Earth and, therefore, forms the virtue of human nature. These two are one and the same thing. Those who follow the Way of Heaven and have no cause for regret can be said to have "the virtue of Heaven"; those who follow the desire of nature without any amissness can be said to have "the virtue of nature." The desires of nature are the signs of the natural. The virtue of nature is conducive to the attainment of necessity *(pi-jan)*.[58] What is conducive to the attainment of necessity conforms to and perfects what is natural of Heaven and Earth. This is called the utmost attainment of the natural.

The *Ta Ya* [Greater Odes] and the *Sung Kao* of the *Shih Ching* [Book of Poetry] says:

> Heaven gives birth to the multitude of the people and causes all things to be organized according to order and regularity. The people are endowed with good nature, and they consequently like good virtues.

All the rules of action and of maintaining dignity are those utmost of the natural and are things with which people are endowed. The natural is distributed among all the daily affairs and doings of the people; necessity is that by conforming to which people may attain the middle way and acquire natural virtues and, therefore, make themselves known as paradigms of virtue under heaven. When a man knows what constitutes the natural, then he comprehends the principles of the formation and transformation of Heaven and Earth; when a man knows what constitutes the necessary, he comprehends the virtue of Heaven and Earth. Hence, [Mencius] says, "Knowing his nature, one knows Heaven." When a man achieves knowledge of the nature of Heaven and man and their virtues, his mind will be illuminated. Hence, Mencius teaches of the "fulfillment of one's mental capabilities to the utmost."

Mencius says:

> It is due to nature that the mouth desires sweet taste; the eye, beautiful colors; the ear, pleasant sounds; the nose,

fragrant odors; and the four limbs, ease and rest. But there is necessity in these natural tendencies, and the superior man does not say of his pursuit of them, "It is my nature." It is owing to necessity that there should be an exchange of love between father and son, an observance of righteousness between ruler and subject, attention to ceremony between guest and host, a presence of knowledge in the wise, and a fulfillment of the Heavenly Way by the sage. But there is nature in these ethical prescriptions. The superior man does not say of his cultivation of them, "It is the necessity."[59]

What comprises the natural endowments of things and follows its own course of action is called nature. When there is any delimitation on the nature of things, we term as necessity what makes the delimitation possible. What comprises the natural endowments of things and follows its own course of action, though it is called nature, also has its necessity. Hence, the superior man should not indulge in the gratification of his desires because his desires follow the course of nature. But when there is delimitation upon the natural endowments of things, though the delimitation is due to necessity, this delimitation has its own *natural* course to follow. Hence, the superior man should not abandon his pursuit of what is natural in things regarding the delimitations of things imposed by necessity.

The *Book of Changes* says in its *Great Appendixes*:

> The nature [of man], having been completed and being continually preserved, is the gate of all good courses and righteousness.

Things as created by the five activating forces and the *yin* and *yang* are pure, good, and upright [balanced or uncrooked], for they are the origin of the nature of things. Because of this, there is no process of an event or no capability of a man that does not exhibit the way of righteousness. For this, there is no other reason but that things do not lose the uprightness *(chih)*[60] of their natures. But since people do not know how to preserve this virtue of uprightness, few men follow the way of the superior man.

The *Doctrine of the Mean* says:

> What Heaven has given in a man is called nature; following this nature is called the Way of Man; cultivating this Way is called instruction.[61]

What Heaven has given is nothing else than the Way of Heaven. But why is it called "What Heaven has given"? The "*Pên-ming*" [Original Destiny] in the *Ta Tai Li Chi* [*Record of Rites* by the Greater Tai] provides the answer:

> What is formed in a thing through the distribution of the Way of Heaven, we call the necessity of that thing; what gives use to the unity of a thing, we call the nature of that thing.

The distribution of the Way of Heaven is that of the five activating forces and the *yin* and *yang*. For the Way of Heaven is the way of the five activating forces and the *yin* and *yang*. A thing acquires its nature by acquiring a part of the five activating forces and the *yin* and *yang*. Things can acquire only part of some of the five activating forces and the *yin* and *yang*; only human beings can acquire part of all of them. Whether only part of some or part of all is acquired is determined at the stage of the initial production of things. Although human beings can acquire part of all of the five activating forces and the *yin* and *yang,* each man differs from another with respect to the degree of brightness, darkness, thickness, and thinness of his share. There are also often cases in which people acquire only a part of some [not all] of the good qualities of the five activating forces and the *yin* and *yang,* though what they lack therefrom may be perfected. Herein lies the difference between the nature of man and the nature of things. And because the *Ta Hsüeh* [Great Learning] has in mind the distribution of nature into individual things, it says, "What Heaven has given is called nature."

When we inquire into the causes of the desires of our ears, eyes, and all other bodily organs, we find that they have their nature in accordance with the Way of Heaven.

The Way of Man is such that, when a man has life, he must have those things that will nurture him. Benevolence will produce all the myriad things of the world; propriety will determine the relationships of all sorts of things; and righteousness will rectify the acts and movements of all things. All this is due to the virtue of Heaven and Earth, from which the Way of Man is also established. Since all these come out of nature, it is said that "Following the nature is called the Way."

Because the five activating forces and the *yin* and *yang* are the activities *(shih)* and capabilities of Heaven and Earth, they are in accord with the virtue of Heaven and Earth. When the activities of man are in accord with the virtue of Heaven and Earth, it is easy to detect the nature of Heaven and Earth in his actions. When the activities of man are not in accord with the virtue of Heaven and Earth, he will pursue his own desires to the detriment of benevolence, propriety, and righteousness. When the capacities of man are in accord with the virtue of Heaven and Earth, it is easy for him to be motivated by Heaven and Earth to perform specific actions. When the capacities of man are far from being in accord with the virtue of Heaven and Earth, he will fail to realize that he must not follow the way of benevolence at the expense of propriety and righteousness; or he will fail to realize that he must not follow the ways of propriety and righteousness at the expense of benevolence.[62] All these result from the fact that, in exemplifying the Way, man loses sight of the principle of the middle way and uprightness. The superior man is aware of this and carefully investigates it: he wants to make the desires of human beings to conform to benevolence, propriety, and righteousness. He also wants to make the fulfillment of benevolence without impinging upon propriety and righteousness; and of propriety and righteousness without adversely affecting benevolence. That is why it is said that "cultivating the Way is called instruction."

The *Doctrine of the Mean* says:

A man's character is to be cultivated by cultivating the Way of Heaven. And the Way of Heaven is to be cultivated by cultivating benevolence. Benevolence is the distinguishing mark of humanity, and the most important aspect of benevolence is in loving relatives. Righteousness is performing what is proper, and the most important aspect of righteousness is in honoring the worthy. The measure of love due to relatives and the degree of reverence due to the worthy are produced by the principle of propriety.[63]

Being benevolent, one is able to love his relatives; being righteous, one is able to honor the worthy; being proper, one therefore knows the measure of love due to relatives and the degree of reverence due to the worthy. When one attains benevolence, he will acquire the ability to love relatives; when one attains righteousness, he will acquire the ability to revere the worthy; finally, when one attains propriety, he will acquire the ability to love his relatives in correct measure and to show reverence to the worthy to the correct degree without ever erring.[64] "To cultivate one's character by cultivating the Way of Heaven" is possible because the Way of Heaven comes from one's person. "To cultivate the Way of Heaven by cultivating benevolence" is possible because only when one acquires the three qualities of benevolence, righteousness, and propriety will he acquire the Way of Heaven.

The *Book of Changes* in its *Great Appendixes* says:

It is due to the facility with which *ch'ien* [the creative force] performs its function of creating and ordering things that *ch'ien* becomes known; it is due to simplicity that *k'un* [the preservative force] exhibits the capacity for preserving things. He who attains this simplicity of *k'un* will be easily followed.[65]

In using the term *"yi"* (easiness) to signify the way of *ch'ien*, the author of the passage above has in mind the principle of creative productivity and the principle of benevolence. In using the term *"chien"* (simplicity) to signify the way of *k'un*,[66] the author of the passage has in mind the principle of order and reason and the principle of wisdom. One who is benevolent is without selfishness. Being without selfishness, he will be devoid of all doubts and therefore can easily acquire knowledge. Acquiring knowledge, he will readily be acquainted with truth.[67] Being acquainted with truth, he will endure long in his pursuit of it. Enduring long, he acquires the virtue of the worthy. If he were not benevolent in the first place, how could he acquire these qualities? The wise man is not sophisticated. Being unsophisticated, he will act without serving any presupposed purpose and therefore is capable of attracting followers easily. Being capable of being easily followed, he will be able to make achievements. Being able to make achievements, he will be great. Being great, he accomplishes the deeds of the sagacious. If he were not wise in the first place, how could he accomplish the deeds of the sagacious? Therefore, the *Great Appendixes* of the *Book of Changes* says: "With the attainment of such ease and such simplicity, a man naturally masters all principles of reason under heaven." This means that the sage fulfills to the utmost all the principles of benevolence, propriety, and righteousness.

Chapter 2

When things depart from the living state, their forms remain but their vital nature *(ch'i)*[1] is dissociated from that of Heaven and Earth. The nature of flowers and trees is such that only when the season and weather are proper for their growth can they reach the stage of ripeness. As for the living beings, which we find flying in the sky and walking or moving on earth, that they live is marked by their having perceptions. But human beings have supreme intelligence[2] that is derived from their mind—mind which is pure, homogeneous, balanced, and upright. The illustrious virtues of this mind accord with those of Heaven and Earth. Hence, those things whose vital natures are not dissociated from the vital nature of Heaven and Earth will always enjoy the living state, and those men whose ways of living[3] are not dissociated from that of Heaven and Earth will always attain sagehood.[4]

[On the one hand,] those who have a strong physique are always strongly fortified; those who have a strong vital nature are always energetic; those who have a strong spirit or will are always adroit or astute; and finally, those who have full knowledge of virtues are always wise. On the other hand, those whose vitality exceeds the mean are always beyond the control of temperance; those whose spirit exceeds the mean[5] are always artificial and deranged and cannot conform to the principles of reason;[6] those who have doubts about virtues[7] are always foolish. Therefore, we may also conclude that for the perfecting and cultivating of oneself, it is more important to have one's vital nature nourished than to have one's bodily form nourished; and it is more important to have one's spirit *(shên)*[8] nourished than to have one's vital nature nourished.

Thus, a superior man has a coherent reason and a heart full of peace, and his nature *(hsing)*[9] will receive its proper nourishment just as the sky imbibes of the sunlight after the rain clouds have been dispersed.[10]

Man has knowledge of the heavenly virtue *(t'ien-tê-chih-chih)*.[11] But he also has innate desires of the ears, the eyes, and other bodily organs, all of which can be manifested in one's natural endowments. Since they all come from Heaven, they are called "nature."[12] The knowledge of heavenly virtue is endowed in man's internal nature and is equal or comparable to the creative and reproductive powers of Heaven and Earth. The desires of the ears, the eyes, and other bodily organs are received in proper portion that cannot be exceeded. Therefore, the disposition to do the right things *(yi)*[13] can be compared to the day's capacity for shedding light, for it represents the virtue of Heaven; while bodily desires can be compared to the night's capacity for bringing darkness, for it follows the virtue of Earth. The five colors, the five sounds, the five smells, and the five tastes[14] are the norms of Heaven and Earth relative to the senses; joy, anger, sorrow and happiness, love, resentment, cares and misgivings, irascibility and indignation, fear and melancholy, the desires for food and for sex, enduring moodiness and rampant feelings of misfortune, grief and exaltation, likes and dislikes—these are all due to nature at the very beginning of its formation and are therefore called the Way.[15]

Through the refined elements of mind, one achieves the power of knowing. Through the power of knowing, one may advance to the stage of supreme intelligence.[16] Then whenever outer events occur, our mind responds to them in such a way that the response accords with the principles of righteous disposition *(tao-yi)*.[17] Knowledge that enables us to respond to outside events in accordance with the principle of righteous disposition is the knowledge of heavenly virtue. Therefore, man exemplifies or represents

the best of Heaven and Earth. The virtue of Heaven and
Earth can indeed be summarized in one word—"benevolence." The virtue of the mind of man can also be epi-
tomized in this term "benevolence." The desires of the
ears, the eyes, and other bodily organs are comprehended
by the mind, but we cannot say that they are what the mind
takes cognizance of because what the mind takes cognizance
of is benevolence. If the ears, the eyes, and other bodily
organs can comprehend the benevolence of the mind, then,
from the mind to the bodily organs, all is benevolence.[18]
With his mind acquiring regularity,[19] the superior man
observes the presence of benevolence in his having perceptions. Similarly, with his bodily organs acquiring the
state of harmony, the superior man observes the presence
of benevolence in his desires.

The *Chuan*[20] says:

> The fine and bright parts of the mind are called *hun* and
> *p'o*.[21]

All things that have life have the fine and bright parts in
their minds. When these fine and bright parts acquire the
permeating power of the vital nature *(ch'i)* and subtle intelligence *(ling)*, they are then distinguished as *"p'o"*;
when these fine and bright parts acquire the penetrating
power of the vital nature and become spirit-like, they are
then distinguished as *"hun."* It is said in the *Yüeh Ch'i*
[Record of Music] in the *Li Chi* [Record of Rites]:

> The fine part of *yang* is called *shên* (the penetrating spirit);
> and the fine and bright part of the feminine vital nature is
> called *ling* (the permeating intelligence). *Shên* and *ling* are
> sources of [the vitality of] all things.[22]

Things must have blood and breath before they can
have mind and perception. Because they have mind and perception, they come to have love for life and fear of death; and
because of that, they seek profit and shun harm. Although
the degree of the brightness and dullness of a man's mind
varies widely, depending on the limitation set by the fine

and bright parts of his *hun* and *p'o,* nonetheless, in all cases, man loves life and fears death. [Why?] Because all things with blood and breath are the same in their love of the one and fear of the other. Hence, the most important quality in a man is intelligence [or wisdom] because it enables him to choose the good. If he is able to choose the good, it means that the fine and bright part of his mind has advanced to the stage of supreme intelligence. Benevolence will then dwell within him. Therefore, the power manifested by Heaven and Earth in their work of the formation and transformation is called *"kuei-shên."*[23] The power of Heaven and Earth is manifested in a different way in the creation of life and is called *"hun-p'o."*[24] The *hun* follows the virtue of Heaven because of its quality of light; the *p'o* follows the virtue of Earth because of its quality of darkness. The functioning of the *hun* is active; the functioning of the *p'o* is quiescent. They exhibit the ultimate capabilities of Heaven and Earth. That which has the function of activity manifests itself in giving; that which has the function of quiescence manifests itself in receiving. The Way of Heaven is that of giving; the Way of Earth is that of receiving. That which gives therefore determines what is right and what is wrong; that which receives is passive and submissive. The *p'o* is called the intelligent, and the *hun* is called the spiritual. When the intelligent reaches its utmost, it becomes acute and penetrating; when the spiritual reaches its utmost, it becomes sagely and incisive in perception. When a man acquires the acute and penetrating power of intelligence and attains to the virtues of sageliness and insight, it is appropriate to say that he has become supremely intelligent.

The *Mêng Tzŭ* [Book of Mencius] says:

> Form and color belong to the heaven-conferred nature. But a man must be a sage before he can fulfill the good capacities of his body and form (*Book of Mencius,* 7A. 38).[25]

The blood, breath, mind, and intelligence of man are all acquired from Heaven: the form and color of man are only his exterior. It is from the Way of Heaven that human beings and other things in the world originate. Just as in their modes of operation, the five activating forces and the *yin-yang* may give life or destroy, so they manifest themselves variously in man and things. Therefore, although man and things depend upon the five activating forces and the *yin-yang* for their being, the color and form they derive from them may be partial or whole, thick or thin [in generous or slight amounts], superior or inferior, able or incapable, fine or coarse, pure or defiled, stupid or bright. Multifariously and all-pervasively, their influence extends [through the universe] and gives rise to an ever-increasing number of creatures. Some cover immense areas and consist of huge numbers; others quite otherwise; some are gigantic in size, and others quite insignificant. Form and color are derived from the five elements *(wu-hsing)* and the *yin-yang* in this manner. All these qualities are distributed variously according to the Way.[26] When things are treated in accordance with their natures, there will be peace and order; if used against their natures, great harm will result.

Things differ greatly in their natures, and each displays its varied natural endowments. In the case of man, his natural endowments are imbued with all the powers of Heaven and Earth and partake of all their virtue. He devises tools and makes use of them to control other creatures. He frees them from fear [tames them], but he does not abuse them.[27] Because he knows through his intelligence the nature of creatures that fly in the sky or crawl on earth, he is able to tame and domesticate them. Because he knows the nature of plants and trees, he is a good farmer, who tends to his weeding and pruning, and a good physician, who prescribes according to the properties of the samples. Because his virtue is comparable to the supreme intelligence, the sage is able to imbue all under his rule with benevolence and to lead them in the path of propriety and righteousness.

The *Hung Fan* [Great Norm] in the *Shu Ching* [Book of Documents] says:

There are five things to be paid attention to in one's conduct: the first is appearance; the second, speech; the third, the act of seeing; the fourth, the act of hearing; and the fifth, the act of thinking.[28]

These are the ways in which the Way is manifested in man. [The *Great Norm* continues:]

The virtue of appearance is called reverence; that of speech, conformity [with proper rules]; that of seeing, clarity; that of hearing, distinctness; that of thinking, sagacity.[29]

Thus, when the young meets the old, he knows how to conduct himself and restrain himself properly. And [this need] not result from being trained in proper behavior.[30] Regarding an uncultured person who may not conform to the principles of righteousness, we can question him and put him to silence in his objections against the principles of righteousness.[31] He can be shown the differences between what is good and what is bad. He can be taught to distinguish between what is true and what is false. Indeed, if a man wants to be enlightened, he will surely be thus ultimately enlightened *(huo-jen)*.[32] From this, we know what human nature is. This is what Mencius calls "the innate goodness of human nature."[33] Following the innate goodness of human nature, a man will understand the order of things under heaven. Thus [it is said that] "reverence leads to solemnity in attitude; conformity with rules leads to good government and order among people; clearness of sight leads to wisdom; quickness of hearing leads to resourcefulness; and sagacity leads to sageliness."[34]

Mencius says:

What is that [of] which all men's minds approve? That is the principles of reason and righteousness. The sages only apprehended before me what I and other men agree in approving (*Book of Mencius*, 6A.7).[35]

In Mencius' time, people under heaven did not know that the principles of reason and righteousness[36] belong to one's nature. Hence, they made erroneous statements which harmed the Way and confounded the laws of the ancient [sage-] kings. Then Mencius rose to clarify and defend the principles of reason and righteousness.

Considering the creation of men and things in the world, we find that there are various kinds of things, and these kinds are what determine the great differences in the nature of things. Mencius says:

> All things that belong to the same species bear resemblance to each other. Why should we doubt this in regard to man? We belong to the same kind as the sage (*Book of Mencius,* 6A.7).[37]

Demanding that Kao Tzŭ give an explanation for his belief that "the nature of living is what I call nature" Mencius says, "Is the nature of a dog like that of an ox, and the nature of an ox like that of a man?" (*Book of Mencius,* 6A.3).[38] This is because Mencius speaks of the universal goodness of human nature and does not simply take the nature of man as something to be shared in common by all men. But since men have approximately the same nature, they are all good.[39] To apprehend that the principles of reason and righteousness belong to the nature of man shows why we do not naturally know that the principles of reason and righteousness belong to the nature of man.[40] Therefore, the principles of reason and righteousness are something that belong to the nature of man.[41] Those scholars coming after Mencius sought his true doctrine but have failed to find it. Instead, they use the names of "nature" *(hsing),* denoting by it what is called "reason *(li)*."[42] But this is not acceptable.[43]

Consider the relation of the ears to sounds: all the sounds under heaven seem to sound respectively the same to all human ears, as if all human ears fit perfectly with them. Consider further the relation of the eyes to colors: all the colors under heaven seem to look respectively the same to all human eyes, as if all human eyes fit perfectly with them. Consider also the relation of the nose to smells: all smells under heaven seem to smell respectively the same to all human noses, as if all human noses fit perfectly with them. Finally, consider the relation of the mouth to tastes: all the tastes under heaven seem to taste respectively the same to human tongues, as if all human tongues fit perfectly with them. In short, the functions of the ears, the eyes, the nose, and the tongue are such that when they are in contact with external things, our minds will comprehend the order and regularity governing these things.[44] [Now,] consider the relation of the human mind to the principles of reason and righteousness: all the principles of reason and righteousness under heaven seem to have the same meaning to all human minds, as if all human minds fit perfectly with them. Hence, we may not say that the principles of reason and righteousness are extraneous to the nature of man: they are [intrinsic to] his nature. The ears can discriminate the various sounds under heaven; the eyes can discriminate the various colors under heaven; the nose can discriminate the various smells under heaven: the tongue can discriminate the various tastes under heaven. Similarly, the human mind can comprehend the various principles of reason and righteousness under heaven. Man has acquired all his natural endowments and capabilities from heaven. Mencius says:

> It is not due to men's natural endowments by Heaven that they are thus different.

He continues:

> From the feelings proper to human nature, we see that human nature is constituted for doing what is good. This is then called the good nature of man. If a man does what is not good, the fault cannot be found in his natural endowments (*Book of Mencius,* 6A.6).

It is only from the point of view of the natural endowments and capabilities[45] that we can definitely determine the goodness of human nature. In respect to their endowments, the difference between an average man and a sage is not so great as that between things [presumably, animals and inanimate objects in nature] and men. Things [in general, including animal] do not have sufficient endowments to enable them to comprehend the uprightness and integrity of Heaven and Earth; they, therefore, do not have self-restraint.[46] They merely pursue the course that nature places within their reach, and no others. But, in the case of man, he has the knowledge of the virtue of Heaven and is also capable of fulfilling the heavenly virtues of uprightness and integrity. What he naturally does accords with the concordance of Heaven and Earth, and those acts which he must perform, such as his duties to other men, accord with the regularity of Heaven and Earth; hence, what he must perform is nothing more than what he naturally would do. The natural happenings of things cannot be compared to this.

When Mencius speaks of the goodness of human nature, he bases his statement on his investigation of the natural inclinations of man's endowments and capabilities and thus holds that which has restraint or self-control within human nature is good.[47] Kao Tzŭ says, "[Man's] nature is neither good nor bad." He says this because he does not notice the great difference between man and things in general and therefore generalizes that all are the same in respect to what is natural to them. Kao Tzŭ's assertion that "[Man's] nature is neither good nor bad" also means that when things in general remain at rest and thus are in a natural state their essences or spiritual state *(shên)*[48] are mostly empty; and that this is the ultimate way of life. He also believes that when things [including men] move toward the good or the non-good they deviate from the ultimate way of life. Therefore, he concludes that "The nature of living is what I call nature."[49] When Mencius comes to question Kao Tzŭ regarding this, Kao Tzŭ does not have a clear idea of the meaning of Mencius' words and therefore remains silent. But he is forced to see the extreme difference between man and things, because man possesses intelligence while other things or beings do not. [He is also forced to see that, according to Mencius' example,] dogs and oxen are of radically different species and cannot be taken as

identical in their natures. It is only those persons like
Hsün Tzŭ and Kao Tzŭ who arbitrarily maintain that
nature is but the natural endowments and capabilities of
physical organs who fail to discern the presence of the
principles of reason and righteousness in the nature of
men. Hsün Tzŭ believes that men who have blood and
breath, and mind and intelligence, must be taught the
principles of reason and righteousness. This is a reversal
of right reasoning that causes him to conclude that man's
nature is bad.[50] Hence, Hsün Tzŭ comes to advance his
doctrine of the pursuit of learning moral principles and of
cultivating one's personality. Kao Tzŭ, in comparison,
thinks that the most worthy man does not have desires and
thus remains in an inactive state, therefore, preserving his
nature of being good or not good; and Kao Tzŭ considers
this to be the ultimate state attainable by man. Regarding
the man who is inferior,[51] Kao Tzŭ thinks that it is necessary to appeal to the principles of reason and righteousness
to have his desires kept in bondage in order to prevent him
from doing things that are not good. Hsün Tzŭ's doctrine
that the principles of reason and righteousness are extraneous to the conditions and capabilities of the nature of man
is one which the Confucian scholars have never heard of
before. But Kao Tzŭ's doctrine that nature is the only thing
that matters, that it is something to which the principles
of reason and righteousness are extraneous, is a heresy that
will only harm the Way *(hai-tao)*.[52]

Broadly speaking, there are three doctrines whose
ideas concerning man's nature greatly differ from those of
the *Yi Ching* [Book of Changes], the *Lun Yü* [Analects],
and the *Book of Mencius*. [First,] there is the doctrine that
considers man's nature to consist of the desires of the ears,
the eyes, and other bodily organs; it, therefore, recommends
that the principles of reason and righteousness govern man
[and his desires]. [Second,] there is the doctrine that considers man's nature to consist of perceptions *(chüeh)*; it,
therefore, claims that the spiritual is the foremost element
in human nature and that this spiritual element is empty

and follows the course of spontaneity, while reasons and desires come only after these. [Third,] there is the doctrine that considers man's nature to consist of reason and holds that it is by having desires and feelings that man is led into bias and selfishness.⁵³ These three doctrines disparage what they have included in man's nature and value what they have excluded from it. The first doctrine emphasizes only the value of the spiritual and assumes the priority of the existence of the spiritual to that of the physical [the body and the form], showing that the advocates of this doctrine are not aware that the essential vital nature of life is the substance, the fine part of which is exhibited in the form of the spiritual. Again, this doctrine assumes that since a man has body and form he must have desires; hence, that he must go beyond his body and form, recognize death and life as being the same, and rid himself of all feelings and desires in order that he may put his spirit to rest, destroy all distinctions between right and wrong, and abandon all thinking and misgivings.⁵⁴ This is the Way in which, he considers, man can speak of the natural source and its spontaneity *(tzŭ-jan)*.⁵⁵ [Another criticism can also be made that] the advocates of this doctrine do not know that to return to what is necessary in a man's life is the very epitome of naturalness because man will attain both movement and rest; that is, his spiritual element will attain repose as a matter of course.

Doctrines centered around the thesis that man's nature is either desire or feeling have flourished since the time of Mencius. But it was Mencius who corrected these doctrines by reminding us that we were not taking sufficient account of reason and righteousness. When the mind arrives at the principles of regularity and when the ears, eyes, and other bodily organs obtain the harmony that befits them, the mind will be pure, good, balanced, and upright: these [attributes of the mind] are called the principles of reason and righteousness. Thus, reason and righteousness are nothing else than what human minds share in common. But how do human minds have something to share in common?

Human minds are such that where their insights rest, they make the distinctions between the right and the wrong with precision and correctness: and this is what is meant by reason and righteousness. If one holds that reason is the only power possessed by the nature of man and that reason will be deteriorated by the presence of the bodily form and vital nature, it is because he does not see how the name "reason" is given to the nature of man. The doctrine that human desires and feelings lead to biases and self-interests is implicit in Hsün Tzŭ's assertion that man's nature is bad. But Hsün Tzŭ sees those biases and selfishness merely as the results of having a loss of balance and integrity; he does not see man's nature as having [its intrinsic] balance and integrity. Moreover, when we have verified that bodily form and vital nature originate from Heaven and when we have comprehended the full virtue of the five activating forces and the *yin* and *yang*, we know that bodily form and vital nature are not selfish desires. What Mencius says about the goodness of the nature of man is this: man's natural endowments and original capabilities are good. It is only when they stray from their inherent virtues *(pên-jan chih-tê)*[56] that they may consciously lose their goodness. If this is so, it is what Mencius refers to as "to give away one's conscience [or good heart]" or "to lose one's original heart."[57] Even if one has given away or lost one's good or original heart, one's bodily form and vital nature still originate from Heaven and comprehend the full virtue of the five activating forces and the *yin* and *yang* and, therefore, just as a living thing near death can recover, so may one still recover.[58] Thus, Mencius says:

> There is some growth of the life of goodness day and night and in the calm air of the morning, just between night and day. The mind feels in a very small degree those desires and aversions that are proper to humanity (*Book of Mencius,* 6A.8).[59]

In view of this idea—that the liking and aversions proper to humanity are present even in the man least influenced by his vital nature—the superior man will not lay blame on his bodily form and his vital nature.[60]

Mencius says:

> The function of ears and eyes is not thinking, [for the ears and eyes] are liable to be obscured by things affecting them. When one thing comes into contact with another, it simply leads its ways. But the function of the mind is to think. By thinking, the mind gets the right view of things; but when it neglects to think, it fails to get the right view of things. These functions—of the sense and the mind—are what Heaven has given us. Let a man first lay hold of the greater part or his nature, and the smaller part will not be able to take [the greater part] from him (*Book of Mencius,* 6A.16).[61]

The natural endowments of man receive the full powers and partake of the virtue of Heaven and Earth. Are not these natural endowments already expressed in man's capacity for thinking? Sincerity[62] is the ultimate to which a man can attain in fulfilling the virtue of Heaven and Earth. Thinking of sincerity is already an act of seizing the greater [and nobler] part of one's nature. It is not the function of the ears and the eyes to think, and, before external things enter into contact with them, they are empty of excitations and are harmonious and natural; this is all there is to be known about the nature of the ears and the eyes. But the function of the mind is quite different. All men have the knowledge of heavenly virtue rooted in their minds; this is called "the enlightenment of intelligence from the reflection of a sincere mind."[63] But when one's thinking is upright and truthful, when one thereby attains the virtue of Heaven, then one's mind will not be obscured or led astray by external things; this is called "the attainment of sincerity from the enlightenment of intelligence."[64] [About the sense-organs,] the ears are able to hear; the eyes, to see; the nose, to smell; and the tongue, to taste because, when external things have contact with them, they [the sense-organs] are prepared for them and hence are able to receive them. The mind, however, is very refined and bright and, when cultivated, will achieve the state of supreme intelligence. That is why the mind governs the functions of the ears, the eyes, and other bodily organs.

Good sounds are naturally received by the ears as fit; good colors are received by the eyes as fit; good smells are received by the nose as fit; and good tastes are received by the tongue as fit. All the desires of the ears, the eyes, and other bodily organs are such that if these organs do not receive what befits them they will lack their nurture. The act of causing these organs to receive what befits them is what is called "nourishing the smaller part [of one's nature]." In contrast, reason and righteousness are things which are received by the mind as fit, and it is these qualities [constituting temperence] that restrain the desires of the ears, the eyes, and other bodily organs. If the mind does not receive what befits it, it will lack its nurture. Hence, to cause the mind to receive what befits it is called "nourishing the greater part [of one's nature]." [As Mencius says:] "How rare are the parts of a man that are different from the beasts?" (*Book of Mencius,* 4B.19). Even the natures of dogs and oxen are such that when their vital natures are not deranged or perturbed they are self-contained, empty of excitations, natural, and harmonious. But when their natures are moved or perturbed, their minds become obscured by external things and hence wander in a confused manner. When a man does not seek to make his mind unobscured by the external things, but instead hates the external things because they tempt him and therefore is forced to guard himself against them, could this be said to be what "constitutes the distinction between a man and an animal?" It is hence no wonder that Lao Tan and Chuang Chou[65] speak of the importance of having no desires, while the superior man [of the Confucian or Mencian persuasion] speaks of the importance of having no obscurity in one's mind or nature. To advocate the doctrine of having no desires, one must take the quietude [and therefore the extinction] of all desires as the ultimate good. But the superior man [in the Confucian sense] judges the values of movement and rest or quietude only in the light of the norm of benevolence. Man does have desires, and it is true that it is easy for these desires to go to extremes. To have either of these things happen is to oppose oneself to the principles of uprightness and integrity of the heavenly virtue. Thus, we must let our mind attain the heavenly virtue and become endowed with the principles of uprightness and integrity so that our desires will not go to the extremes but will be properly restrained by our mind, even at the risk of depriving the heavenly virtue [that is] truthful of our mind. Thus, Mencius says, "For nourishing the mind, there is nothing better than to make one's desires few" (*Book of Mencius,* 7B.35).

When Yü[66] wanted to conduct the flood to the sea, he let the water flow through the fields. Just so, as the superior man wants to conduct his desires into the right channel, he must let them go in conformity with the principles of reason and righteousness. If the man who is charged with the task of controlling the flood were to take action to prevent the flood from running through the fields, he would find himself in a situation where he would stop the flow from running to the east only at the cost of causing it to run to the west. Even worse than that may happen: he would find the flood breaking the embankment and flowing in all directions, which would only end in a deluge in which no one could be of any help. Similarly, if one were to want to rule oneself in order to rule others, if he were to resort only to preventing his own and others' desires from following their natural course of functioning and gratification, he would find himself in the same situation [as was the man who attempted to control the flood]. Even if one were capable of seeking quietude by eradicating all natural desires, he, as a superior man, would not take this as the right way of treating desires. What the superior man will do in order to rule himself and others is to cause his desires to conform to the principles of reason and righteousness and to prevent other people and their desires from opposing these principles. [In the matter of controlling desires,] this is all that a superior man will do.

Chapter 3

That man cannot often fulfill his natural endowments is due to either of two causes: one is "selfishness" *(ssŭ)*[1] and the other is that his intelligence is beclouded *(pi)*[2] [by external things]. Selfishness, when it arises in one's heart, leads to indulgence in one's personal desires; when it plays a part in politics, it entails partisanship; when it affects one's actions, it results in wrongdoings; when it arises in matters of human relationships, it takes the form of unreasonableness and deceit. In the end, selfishness has its root in the satisfaction of one's private desires and interests. In the other case, [that is,] when the mind is beclouded by external things, the mind becomes confused; when political matters are similarly beclouded, the men involved in them become partial; when the beclouding is manifested in one's behavior, the behavior has already become absurd; when the obscuration of intelligence appears in matters of human relationships, these matters run counter to the principles of reason and are marked by stupidity. In the end, the beclouding of intelligence has its root in the beclouding of intelligence by one's self. What runs counter to the principles of reason has its causes in deceit; what is marked by stupidity has its cause in willfulness lacking in introspection; a deceitful man will do things according to his willfulness. If a selfish man is content with his selfishness, treating it as an integral part of his nature, he may be said to do violence to himself.[3] If a man whose intelligence is beclouded does not seek to enlighten himself with truth, he may be said to have abandoned himself to ignorance and stupidity. When a man has done violence to himself by embracing selfishness and abandoning himself to ignorance, it is difficult to speak of goodness with him, and he will finally become a man without goodness. [But] we certainly cannot blame a man's natural endowments for this.

In order to get rid of selfishness, one can do nothing better than to strengthen one's compassion for other people;[4] while trying to free oneself from the bondage resulting from the beclouding of intelligence, one can do nothing better than to pursue learning. If one wants to acquire the guiding principle of life, the virtues to follow are none other than loyalty and faithfulness [i.e., loyalty to what is good and faithfulness to what one can rightly do]. If one wants to know how to conduct oneself and whether to proceed with one's present conduct, the virtue that he needs to follow consists only of the understanding of the good. Hence, what are called the heavenly virtues *(t'ien-tê)* are three: benevolence *(jên)*, propriety *(li)*, and righteousness *(yi)*.[5] These are the major headings of the good and the norms by which we regulate our conduct and evaluate the rightness of our actions. About the ethical ordering of human relationships, when we allege one of these norms, we find ourselves alleging all three simultaneously. If we fail in our performance of even one of these virtues, we shall not attain the ultimate goodness offered only by the three.

There are three virtues—called the virtues of high attainment—that are essential for the perfection of one's nature: wisdom, benevolence, and courage.[6] There are also three virtues that, if followed, will enhance our performance of the three other virtues: loyalty, faithfulness, and compassion. Loyalty consists in one's doing what one is capable of doing.[7] Faithfulness lies in fulfilling what one has promised to do. Compassion consists in justly rendering to other people what is due to them, as by equalizing the distribution of things among people. Being loyal, one can advance to the practice of benevolence; being faithful, one can advance to the practice of righteousness; being compassionate regarding other people, one can advance to the practice of propriety.

Benevolence is the prototype of all virtues,[8] which, if practiced, can enable one to know the truth in a thousand things and to share the feeling of all people under heaven. Hence the virtue of loyalty is but a corollary to that of benevolence. The virtue of righteousness involves a knowledge of what befits humanity, the practicing of which enables one to share the same view of things of one's fellow men; and to help things become themselves and grow toward perfection. Hence, the virtue of faithfulness is a corollary to that of righteousness. But the principles of propriety are where the heavenly order resides; they prevail among all human beings and their relationships so that people under heaven may live in mutual peace; by the principles of propriety, no one will fail to fulfill his obligations. Hence, the virtue of compassion is merely a corollary to the principles of propriety.

Loyalty resembles the principle of easiness *(yi)*;[9] compassion regarding other people resembles the principle of simplicity *(chien)*.[10] But by being faithful and undeceitful, one also approaches the principle of easiness; and by being faithful and constant, one also approaches the principle of simplicity. When properly cultivated and attained to their highest possible degree, these three traits of loyalty, compassion, and faithfulness are such that the man who possesses them will have acquired the virtues of benevolence and wisdom. Those who are benevolent and wise will be unselfish and free from bias and beclouding of intelligence. When one acquires the power of the creativity of life, he will be benevolent. But when a man does the contrary and, therefore, harms the principle of benevolence, he is said to be selfish. When one's mind acquires the principles of order and reason, he is then wise; but when one is separated from the principles of order and reason and, hence, is weak in his judgment and insight, he is described as being beclouded in his mind.

When a man takes his own opinion *(chih)* as wisdom *(chih)*[11] and asserts that his opinion can apply to all sorts of behavior without being unreasonable, the Way will not prevail in the world.[12] Those people whose nature is essentially good will believe in the righteousness of their acts and assert that their benevolence, kindness, loyalty, and faithfulness are already known and manifest.[13] When they do this, the ultimate nature of the Way is not illuminated. Hence, it is clear that a superior man sees great value in controlling himself. A person who is solitary and cannot fill his heart with goodness is called a "self." Those who let the "self" becloud the mind are separated from the good; those who are separated from the good are therefore separated from their fellow men. When a man is not separated from the good, he will achieve the virtue of benevolence, realize the virtue of righteousness, and know the [Way of] Heaven. Hence, everything has its principle of order and reason for being and becoming, and every act has its principle of righteousness and propriety: one may appeal to the ancient teachings to testify to these truths, on the basis of which one can accommodate oneself to various times and situations and achieve an appropriate harmony. The man who holds these truths clearly in his mind will know how to deport himself by basing his conduct on these principles. A superior man will always think of the virtue of benevolence; even when he is alone. When he speaks in public, he will always speak in conformity to the principle of righteousness. All his acts, from beginning to end, will be in accord with the principles of propriety. In attaining the principles of propriety, the superior man will never be imprecise in his observance of the virtue of righteousness; by being precise in his observance of righteousness, he will not fail to achieve the virtue of benevolence. When he achieves benevolence and fulfills the duties of a man in relation to other men, he will become a sage. The virtues of being "easy," "simple," and reaching the supreme good are the attainments that the sage desires to share with all people under heaven for a thousand generations.

The *Lun Yü* [Analects] says:

> By nature, men are nearly alike; by practice, they get to be wide apart. It is only the wise of the highest grade and the dull of the lowest grade who cannot be changed (*Analects*, 17.2).

Men and things differ extremely in their natures and constitutions, even when judged according to their common attributes on a very general level; men themselves are similar in their nature, and it is only after the influence of practice and habit that they grow far apart [amongst themselves], even when judged according to their differences on a very general level. All those things that belong to the same kind are in general alike. It is only in the wise of the highest grade and in the dull of the lowest grade that their differences of brightness and fullness in intelligence can be said to be the results of birth or of a hereditary nature—not habit or practice. But in speaking of the wise of the highest class and the stupid of the lowest class, we are aware of their natures and of the fact that their natures cannot change. This is why we speak of them as we do. But "being incapable of change" is not the same as "being incapable of being changed."[14] Therefore, the *Analects* says:

> Those who are born with the knowledge of goodness are men of the highest grade. Those who learn and so know goodness are the next. Those who are forced to learn because of needs are next to these. As for those who are dull and yet do not learn, they are the men of the lowest grade (*Analects*, 16.9).

Hence, the superior man is very cautious about his habits or practices lest they have a bad influence over him; hence, he values learning highly.

The *Chung Yung* [Doctrine of the Mean] says:

> The Way should not be deserted for an instant. If it could be deserted, it would not be the Way. On this account, the superior man does not wait till he sees things to be cautious or till he hears things to be apprehensive.

The *Doctrine of the Mean* also says:

> It is said in the *Shih Ching* [Book of Poetry]: "Looked at in
> your room, be there as free from shame as if exposed to the
> light of heaven." Therefore, the superior man, even when
> he is not moving, has a feeling of reverence, and even when
> not speaking, has a feeling of truthfulness.

It is by the bodily organs of seeing and hearing that we
keep in contact with external things. In speaking of movement [of a man], we mean that the man [or the superior
man] responds to the external stimulus. Now, if, on the
one hand, the Way comes from one's person, then how can
one ever set oneself apart from the Way? On the other hand,
if, before external things exert their influence over a person,
that person opens his mind and does not exercise any control
over himself, he will certainly lose the Way altogether.
Being pure, virtuous [or worthy], and upright, one will
follow the principles of the Way. When external things exert
their influence over us, we seldom remain at rest. But then
we often stray from the principles of purity, virtuousness,
and uprightness because of the lack of control over our
desires. Hence, how can we not always worry about our
possible carelessness in matters of moral motivation?

The *Doctrine of the Mean* says:

> There is nothing more visible than what is secret and nothing
> more manifest than what is minute. Therefore the superior
> man is watchful over himself, even when he is alone.[15]

The *Doctrine of the Mean* also says:

> It is said in the *Book of Poetry*: "Although [the fish] sinks
> and lies at the bottom, it is still quite clearly seen." There-
> fore, the superior man examines his heart that there may be
> nothing wrong there and that he may have no badness in
> his mind. What the superior man cannot be equalled is
> simply this: his self-examination that other men cannot see.[16]

To be alone means that one encompasses the right principles within one's heart and that one has displayed them
in his performances: wherein lie things that other men

cannot see. All things that are visible have their beginnings in secret. All things that are to take action have their beginnings in being alone.[17] Those people who very often lose their virtues make too much of a show themselves. This is because when they begin to take action by their intentions they have already strayed from the right principles. Since the beginning of their action is a wrongful one, the whole action leads to the wrong consequences. A superior man, therefore, will always rectify his intentions before he sets himself to act; hence, how could his actions be wrong? This is what is meant by saying that one knows how to be watchful over oneself.

The *Doctrine of the Mean* says:

> While there are no stirrings of mirth, anger, sorrow, or joy, the mind may be said to be in a state of equilibrium *(chung)*. When those feelings have been stirred and they act in their due degree, the mind may be said to be in a state of harmony *(ho)*. This equilibrium is the great root [from which grow all human actions] under heaven, and this harmony is the universal Way which all should pursue. Attaining equilibrium and harmony, we can be certain that a happy order will prevail throughout heaven and earth and that all things will be nourished and will flourish.[18]

A man who has his own desires and who also takes into consideration the desires of others is benevolent. A man who has his own feelings[19] and who also takes into consideration the feelings of others is wise. A man should hate selfishness because it does harm to the virtue of benevolence, and he should also hate the beclouding of intelligence by external things because it does harm to intelligence. When a man is neither selfish nor beclouded [in his intelligence], his mind will remain pure and clear; this is a state of supreme illumination *(shên-ming)*. When a mind is still and does not move, it will be pure and attain the perfection of heavenly virtue; hence, the state of equilibrium is said to be "the great root from which grow all human actions in the world"; when a man is in action [as affected by external things] in such a way that his action also remains pure and never leads to selfishness or to the beclouding of intelligence, this way is then said to be the universal Way that all men should pursue in the world. The above observations make it clear that a man's natural endowments and capacities are worthy and that human nature is in no sense bad. When the intelligence of a man is enlightened by sincerity, the principles of righteousness and reason will produce in him a state of equilibrium and harmony. But when a man gains his sincerity from the enlightenment of his intelligence, he will understand the difference between the principles of righteousness and reason and those of equilibrium and harmony; he is thus capable of cultivating himself into a sage.

> It is only he who is sincere that can exist under heaven who can give its full development to his nature. Able to give its full development to his own nature, he can do the same to the nature of other men. Able to give its full development to the natures of other men, he can give their full development to the natures of animals and things *(Doctrine of the Mean)*.

This is how one can arrive at the state of equilibrium and harmony by attaining enlightenment of intelligence from one's sincerity.

> Next to the above is he who cultivates to the utmost the small beginnings of goodness in him. As soon as a man can do this, he is capable of possessing sincerity. As soon as a man has sincerity, his sincerity will become apparent. From being apparent, it will become conspicuous. From being conspicuous, it becomes brilliant. Brilliant, it moves. Moving, it changes. Changing, it transforms *(Doctrine of the Mean)*.[20]

This is how one may arrive at states of equilibrium and harmony: by attaining sincerity from the enlightenment of one's intelligence. When a happy order prevails throughout Heaven and Earth, then none of the things under heaven will fail to obtain regularity in their full development of nature. When all things are nourished, and flourish, then none of the things under heaven will fail to obtain concordance.

The *Doctrine of the Mean* says:

> The superior man reveres virtuous nature and conducts constant inquiry and learning. He seeks to obtain virtue and exhaust learning to their full breadth and greatness, covering every exquisite and minute point of them and raising them to their utmost height and brilliancy so that he may pursue the course of the mean. He cherishes his old knowledge so that he may continually acquire anew. He exerts an earnestness on good nature and honesty in the esteem and practice of propriety.[21]

Those who are imperfect because of the beclouding of their intelligence must be narrow-minded; those who are imperfect because of their selfishness must be mean and perverse. These people, in short, are the opposite of those who are broad-minded in their inquiry and study and who cherish high ideals. Those who seek "to improve their virtuous natures to the full extent of their breadth and greatness" will not let themselves be harmed by the beclouding of their intelligence and, therefore, will be capable of "comprehending all the exquisite and minute points of their inquiry and study"; those who seek "to raise their search to the utmost height and brilliance" will not let selfishness divert their efforts and, therefore, will be capable of pursuing the course of the mean. "To exhaust the minutest and finest point [of one's virtuous nature and learning]," one will therefore be unbeclouded in one's intelligence; "to pursue the course of the mean," one will therefore not be selfish. All men have the beginnings [roots] of being unbeclouded in their intelligence:[22] this can result from the previous knowledge that they have acquired. One may benefit from constant inquiry and study, and one's virtuous nature will be substantiated day by day. Then this result of constant inquiry and study will also become part of one's old knowledge. All men also have beginnings [or roots] of being unselfish:[23] this can result from their generous [earnest and charitable] nature.[24] What a man has gained from his constant inquiry and study and what he has obtained from the day-by-day substantiation of his

virtuous nature will also contribute to his generosity. As a
man cherishes his old knowledge, he may be said to be able
to carry on his study to its utmost breadth and greatness;
as a man exhibits an honest earnestness, he may be said
to be able to "reach the utmost height and brilliancy." "To
esteem and practice all propriety" is the way by which we
may gradually proceed to "the pursuit of the course of the
mean."

The *Doctrine of the Mean* says:

> [A Ruler] wishing to cultivate his character may not neglect
> to serve his parents. In order to serve his parents, he may not
> neglect to acquire a knowledge of men. In order to know
> men, he may not dispense with a knowledge of Heaven.

The superior man cultivates his character by practicing
the virtue of benevolence so that his character will be
perfected; he practices the virtue of benevolence by refining
his sense of righteousness so that his character will be perfected; he practices the virtue of benevolence by refining
his sense of righteousness so that the virtue of benevolence
will come to him; finally, he refines his sense of righteousness by achieving propriety in all his acts so that the principle of righteousness will be completely fulfilled by him.

The *Analects* says:

> A young brother or a son, when at home, should be filial and,
> when abroad, should be respectful to his elders. He should
> be earnest and truthful. He should extend love to all and
> cultivate the friendship of the good. When he has time and
> energy after the performance of these virtues, he should
> employ them in the studies of literature and the arts (*Ana-
> lects,* 1.6).

The *Ta Hsüeh* [Great Learning] lists the following four
items concerning virtue: extend your knowledge to the
utmost; make your heart [or intentions] sincere; rectify
your mind; and cultivate your character. It also lists the
following three: regulate your family; govern well your
state; and bring peace to the world.[25] The youth is one who
performs what he clearly understands and one who should

not be idle in practicing what he has learned from his superiors; hence, he is one who, though he practices virtues, has not yet achieved them. But for those who have assumed the responsibility of the whole world or of the whole nation or of a whole family, we observe what they have done and title the principles which they should follow as those given in the *Great Learning*.[26] A man responsible for a whole family or a whole nation or a whole world must act by himself, and his actions must be determined by his mind, planned by his intentions, and suggested by his intelligence. If no clear discrimination concerning right and wrong, good and evil, or truth and falsehood is made, it is one's lack of intelligence that is to blame. If one tends to support evil and pursue the wrong and does not make a sufficient effort to pursue the good, it is his intentions that are to blame. If one becomes dispirited in the face of challenge and cannot make a choice and is loose and uncontrollable, it is his mind that is to blame. If one is partial-minded and always finds himself in doubt, it is his character that is to blame. Thus the *Yi Ching* [Book of Changes] says:

> The superior man pays regard to the far-distant end and knows the mischief that may be done at the beginning.[27]

If these four defects, or shortcomings, are eliminated, the whole world and the whole nation and family will be well regulated and ordered. It may be asked why the *Great Learning* says: "To extend one's knowledge to the utmost, one must investigate the things of the world." When things come to hand, even the sage will not grasp thoroughly the details of their nature without minute investigation. This shows that it is not easy to decide between right and wrong, and truth and falsehood. The term "investigation" is meant to indicate that one will gain knowledge of the nature of things and will not lose it; and that one then will use one's thinking in a thorough and consistent way without omitting any item. Then, one who thus investigates will have no doubts, and, when he applies what he knows to the problems of the whole world or to the whole nation and the whole family, he will not have regret on account of ignorance: This is what is meant by "one must extend one's knowledge to the utmost."

The *Record of Rites* says in its *Li Yün* [Evolution of Rites]:

> In drinking and eating and sexual activities are found the great and virgin desires of a man.

The *Doctrine of the Mean* says:

> The duties between ruler and subjects, between father and son, between husband and wife, between elder brother and younger, and between those belonging to friendly intercourse are the five duties governing the Way of man under heaven.

Desires in connection with drinking, eating, and sexual activities are desires connected with the nourishment and reproduction of life. It is in connection with these that we know the reason why Heaven and Earth are productive [creative] and reproductive.[28]

Within a family, the relationships between father and son and between elder brother and younger are those of blood.[29] The relationship between husband and wife is one between two halves.[30] In the world or in a nation [or family], a multitude of private wills will lead to confusion and disturbance. Hence, there comes into existence the hierarchy of a ruler and his subjects. Those who understand the way of the relationship between a ruler and his subjects will never find difficulty in conducting successful government. Even when a man is weak and alone in society, he can nevertheless rely upon his virtuous acts for help. When a man is needy and has little assistance, friends come into existence. A friend is one who is always helping. Those who understand the way of making friends and behaving as friends can always help one another and come to one another's assistance when necessary.

All these five relationships are determined from the existence of an individual person and are based on the very principles that guide the creative activity of Heaven and

Earth and that lead to the harmonious ordering and patterning of all things in the world. Thus, those who seek to eliminate the way of creative production and nourishment,
such as those exhibited in the creative and harmonizing
activities of Heaven and Earth and in the five human relationships, will do harm to the Way of Heaven and Earth.
The insignificant people get what they desire, while the
superior men get the virtue of benevolence. [This is the
way in which Heaven and Earth operate.] If a man who
seeks to satisfy his own desires also thinks of seeking to
satisfy the desires of other people, he will then have an
abundance of the virtue of benevolence, more of it than he
can use. If one seeks only to indulge in the pleasure of
satisfying his own desires and neglects the satisfaction of
the desires of others, he will become selfish and hence lack
benevolence. In matters of pursuing pleasure in eating and
drinking, we must value respectfulness and moderation in
satisfying these desires. In matters of pursuing sexual pleasure, we must value circumspection and have a sense of discrimination regarding the different capacities of the male and
the female. And this indicates the importance of propriety.
To value a sense of frugality and a sense of shame and to
understand the importance of temperance and the limitations of one's desires will lead to having no base feelings and
desires. This indicates the importance of the virtue of righteousness. The reason for men's not killing one another is
that they possess feelings of benevolence; the reason for
men's behaving differently from birds and beasts is that
they possess feelings of propriety and righteousness. If men
pay attention only to their own desires and are not benevolent and hence are devoid of the feelings of propriety and
righteousness, then trouble, disaster, danger, and destruction will ensue: they will perish and their names will be
disgraced as fast as the shadow that follows what casts the
shadow and the sound that follows what causes the sound.[31]
As a son, a man must act from his filial piety; as a younger
brother, a man must act from his brotherly love and respect;
as an underling minister [in the government], a man must

act from his loyalty to his ruler; as a friend, a man must act from his sense of responsibility and truthfulness. If a man acts otherwise, he is going against the Way. As a father, a man must act from kindly love; as an edler brother, a man must act from his brotherly love and regard; as a ruler, a man must act from benevolence [for the people]. If he acts otherwise, he is again going against the Way. The ideal of the relationship between father and son points to the existence of the utmost feelings of love and gratefulness; that between older brother and younger brother points to the existence of the utmost feelings of harmony; that between a ruler and his subjects, though comparable to that between father and son regarding the feeling of love and gratefulness that should obtain between them, nevertheless, points to the existence of the utmost feelings of reverence; the perfect or ideal relationship between friends, though comparable to that between elder and younger brothers regarding the feelings of harmony that should obtain between them, nevertheless, points to the existence of the utmost feelings of mutual appreciation and dependence. The perfect or ideal relationship between husband and wife is comparable to that between father and son regarding the feelings of love and gratitude that should obtain between them; it is comparable to that between elder and younger brothers regarding the feelings of harmony that should obtain between them; it is comparable to that between the ruler and his subjects regarding the feelings of reverence that should obtain between them; and, finally, it is comparable to that between friends regarding the feelings of mutual appreciation and dependence that should obtain between them: it, nevertheless, points to the existence of the utmost feelings of discretion [or discrimination between the male and the female].

Filial piety, love for one's older brother, love for one's son, regard for one's younger brother, loyalty toward one's ruler, and a sense of responsibility and truthfulness for one's friend are all the virtues that a benevolent man must possess. The feelings of love and gratitude, of harmony, of reverence, and of friendly companionship are the signs or marks indicating what is natural among human relationships. Failure in trying to practice these virtues to the utmost would only result in a man's separation from other people naturally related to him, in his resenting others or others resenting him and in his feelings and actions being evil and cruel. If men in a society are all perverse against the natural feelings among men, then disaster, calamities, dangers, and destructions will always ensue. Unless one feels that his performance of the virtues of benevolence, propriety, and righteousness has been in no way defective, he cannot be said to be capable of performing these virtues and of performing them to the utmost. If one wants to carry out these virtues and carry them out to the utmost, he must use his intelligence to know them well and to practice them through his feeling of benevolence; and, finally, to persist in using his wisdom and feeling of benevolence for the performance of these virtues with a valiant spirit. In this way, we may expect that he will know that his performance of the virtues of benevolence, propriety, and righteousness has been in any way defective. We need go no further than this. The *Yü Hsia Shu* [Codes of Yü Hsia] says:

> When there is a daily display of three virtues, their possessor could, early and late, regulate and enlighten his family of which he was the head.[32]

Broad-mindedness, tender-heartedness, and compassion are the three virtues [described in the *Shu Ching* (Book of Documents)]. "Broad-mindedness" is used to describe the tolerant attitude of a superior man; "tender-heartedness" is used to describe the superior man's conformity to the right principles; "compassion" is used to describe the truthful, sincere, and simple character of the superior man. Being broad-minded and deferential, a man will discern what is virtuous and what is not. Being tender-hearted and also basing his conduct on solid ground, a man will know how to be upright and will so remain. Being compassionate and respectful, a man will give an appearance of solemnity and authority. Since men possess different capabilities and properties, they will therefore develop virtues of different categories. In contrast to the three mentioned above, we have another triad of virtues: simplicity, firmness of purpose, and energy or determinations of spirit. Simplicity means not being complex or involved; firmness of purpose means the ability to make decisions or resolutions; energy or strong determination of spirit means an unyielding spirit. Being simple and uncorrupt, a man will be strict in matters of making financial profit and will not be idle in his efforts to attain virtues; being firm in one's determination and full of spirit, a man will have feelings of sympathy, pity, and benevolence toward people; being strong in spirit and also righteous, a man will be insistent on right principles and will not act to pervert them. These three virtues are cultivated by the chief of a family so that his family will be well ordered.

The *Codes of Yü Hsia* in the *Book of Documents* says again:

> There is a daily strict and reverent cultivation of six virtues: their possessor could brilliantly conduct the affairs of the state, to which he was the ruler.

Being able to secure good government, being able to inspire obedience of people, and being just—these are the three virtues for a ruler. Together with the virtues of broad-mindedness, tender-heartedness, and compassion, we have then six virtues applicable to a ruler who is also the chief of a family. The above-mentioned three virtues for the ruler may also go together with the virtues of simplicity, firmness of purpose, and strength of spirit, to make six virtues for the ruler who is also a family chief. In speaking of being able to secure good order in government, we mean the ability to obtain the right way of governing; in speaking of being able to inspire obedience in people, we mean the ability to pacify the people with ease; in speaking of being just, we mean the disposition not to be deceitful or to act in disguise. Having the capability to rule and yet remain reverent, [the superior man] will not be amiss in his acts. Having docility of temperament, combined with firmness of mind, he will be able to make the people follow his orders. Being frank and, at the same time, amiable, he will be able to have other men willing to be under his command. These six virtues are those to apply to men in charge of a nation [or a kingdom].

On the basis of the aforementioned three virtues, we may come to know a man and determine to which of these three virtues he is closer than are other men. On the basis of the aforementioned six virtues, we may come to know a man and his usefulness in assuming a public responsibility, by virtue of our knowledge that he has special talents in those matters of government for which he can assume a public responsibility. From ancient times, it has always been difficult to know a man. But by observing a man's behavior on the basis of these three or six virtues, we may come to know his talents and his usefulness. It is said, therefore, that "There are in all nine virtues relating to a man's conduct."[33] By judging the merits of deficiencies of government officers on the basis of these nine virtues, we can find the right persons to be government officers. Hence, it is again said that "When we say that a man possesses virtue, that is as much as to say that he does such and such things."[34] But, as virtues are such that not all of them need to be present in a single man, it is again said that "When such men are all received and employed, the possessors of these nine virtues will all have their services. Then men of a thousand and men of a hundred will fill the offices of the state; the various ministers will emulate one another."[35] This indicates the ultimate way of putting people to the right use in the government.[36]

The *Analects* says:

> The superior man thinks of virtue; the small man thinks of the land of his birth. The superior man thinks of the sanctions of law; the small man thinks of favors and benefits that he may receive from the land (*Analects,* 4.11).

Those who are superior men are conversed in the knowledge of virtues and principles and approve of the codes of law; those who are small men are content with their land and enjoy the favors and benefits it renders them. These four things [i.e., let the superior man think of virtues, and let him think of sanctions of law; let the small men think of land, and let them think of favors and benefits] are the great beginnings of the way to secure able men [for the government] and the great beginnings of the way to govern the people. The *Doctrine of the Mean* has discussed "the reasons why a good government lies in the behavior of good men in the government. Such men are to be got by means of the ruler's own good character." Since ancient times, there has never been a case of being able to make other people follow one without first making oneself a good example to follow. When one knows how to think of good virtues and how to think of the sanctions of law, he will know the way to receive the sage with propriety. The *Book of Changes* says in its *Great Appendixes*:

> The superior man settles himself well in his land and cherishes the virtue of generous benevolence. Hence, he can love [without reserve].

The *Book of Documents* says:

> The superior man benefits by settling people in their land, and all the people will think of him ("Consultations of Kao Tao," *Codes of Yü Hsia*).

It is also said in the *Book of Mencius*:

> If the people do not have a constant material possession, they will not have a fixed heart (*Book of Mencius,* 3A.3).

The *Book of Mencius* also says:

> To dispense a benevolent government to the people, a ruler should be sparing in the use of punishments and fines and make the taxes and levies of produce light. He will see to it that the fields will be ploughed deep; that the weeding, well attended to; and that the able-bodied, during their days of leisure, by cultivating their filial piety, fraternal duty,

faithfulness, and truthfulness, shall thereby serve well, at home, their fathers and elder brothers and, abroad, their elders and superiors (*Book of Mencius,* 1A.5).

It goes on to say that:

> On occasions of death or of moving from one place to another, there will be no quitting the native land. In the fields of a native land, those who belong to the same nine-square render friendly help to one another, in their going out and coming in and in keeping watch and ward; and sustain one another in sickness. Thus the people will be led to live in affection and good neighborhood (*Book of Mencius,* 3A.3).[37]

If the ruler knows how people will treasure their land and value the favors and benefits that they receive therefrom, he will have a way of conducting his government so that people will be governed in good order.

The *Hung Fan* [Great Norm] of the *Book of Documents* says:

> Without partiality and without partisanship, the Way of the King is very broad. Without partisanship and without partiality, the Way of the King is very easy.[38]

This means that a man, acting with other men, should not try to act in a partisan spirit from his own self-interest; he should not be partial in attitude from the beclouding of his mind. If a man is not partial in attitude and, because of this, does not act in a partisan spirit with other men, he will be able to deal with the people under heaven with great public-mindedness *(ta-kung)*.[39] If, however, a man does not act in a partisan spirit with other men and, because of this, is not partial in attitude, he will be able to discriminate [or discern] things in the world with great acumen. The words of the *Great Norm* from the *Book of Documents* follow thus:

> Without perversity and without one-sidedness, the Way of King is right and straight.

"Perversity and one-sidedness" means that a man surreptitiously learns "the art of closing and opening."[40] But this

certainly does not accord with Heaven and Earth about being hard or soft, mobile or still, or manifest and obscure.[41]
   The *Book of Changes* says:

> The great ruler has ordered that, for the purpose of opening a state and transmitting a family, small men should not be employed.[42]

From ancient times, there has not been a single case where a man who is known or regarded as a "small man" has been employed for important offices in the government. When the *Book of Changes* calls this kind of man a "small man," it intends to make a point of his smallness. It shows that a small man is one who pleases his superiors with small profits or favors and prides himself on his small knowledge; and one who obeys the law with seemingly great caution and runs after his master with seemingly great loyalty. But it is only the great ruler who sees deep and knows his smallness and who knows that trouble for the nation or kingdom always begins with the smallness of a small man. Hence, it is said in the *Book of Changes* that:

> [They, the small men, are] sure to throw the states into confusion.[43]

The *Analects* says:

> Fine words and an insinuating appearance are seldom associated with virtue (*Analects,* 1.3; 17.15).

This passage also refers to those who seek the pleasures of their rulers or masters by their faces. In fact, small men possess no feelings of sympathy and pity toward their fellow men; therefore, they avoid saying what is unpleasant to hear. Moreover, to please their ruler or master, they offer what tastes sweet to their ruler, accommodate him by associating with those men whom he respects, and by staying away from those of whom he disapproves. With seemingly great caution and loyalty, they actually do two things: one is "punishment" and the other is "profit-making."[44] In matters of accusations and convictions of the people, the small men will be in great haste to make a careful investigation so that the accused will always be convicted. In matters of collecting taxes, they will never leave untaken even one grain of gold or silver; they will not reduce the amount of tax that they collect; rather, they always increase it, which they feel is small. The laws and items of taxation that had already been abolished are always reinstituted by them for the purpose of collecting more money from the people; and the laws and items of taxation that are set up for temporal use will never be abrogated in order to return to a normal situation. People will therefore become more impoverished day by day and, as a result, the nation will soon perish. The trouble begins with very small things, but the reason for its finally developing into a hopeless extent is that those who, by their pleasing appearance, purposefully insinuate themselves into the favor of their rulers or masters are not noticed—hence, their corrupting influence. Thus, it is difficult to get superior men into government, but it is very easy to get them out. The converse, however, holds for the small man. In other words, the superior men day by day become more suspected by the ruler, while the small men day by day draw closer to him.

The *Ta Ya* [Greater Odes] of the *Book of Poetry* says:

> Let us cherish this center of the country to pacify the four quarters. Let us not let loose the wily and the obsequious to make the unconscientious careful and to repress trespassers and tyrants who have no fear of the Will of Heaven.[45]

This suggests that if small men are entrusted with the responsibility of government, few will abandon their methods of using "tricks" and "cruel punishments." Hence, to guard against the ill effects of the bad characters, we should not let the men who only know flattery and insinuating obedience enter the government. We should also prevent lovers of cruelty and punishment from entering the government because they do not even fear the Will of Heaven; and for which reason, they will do harm to the people. It is owing to the two vices of perversity and deceitfulness that the above is true. All selfish acts that are deceitful have the effect that the man who practices such acts will be tricky in dealing with people and will not have a good heart. A man who is selfish and accordingly becomes perverse will be cruel with regard to people and will have no fear or respect for the Will of Heaven. There is seldom a man, lacking a good heart, who does not become tricky; having no fear [or respect] for the Will of Heaven, a man must then indulge in cruelty.

The *Greater Odes* of the *Book of Poetry* says:

> The unceasing disorder of the people is due to those hy-pocrites who are skilled in intrigue and who cause harm to the people as if their efforts were not equal to their harm. The depravity of the people is brought about by their strenuous competitions. That the people are unsettled is due to the trespassers who prey upon them.[46]

If those who are in office are in general prone to be weak in virtue and good at cheating and perjury, they will bring injury to the people; then the people will also cheat one another; and there will be no end to the process. If those who are in office practice cruelties and compete in suppress-ing people by brute force, then the people will adroitly avoid the perverse treatment by them and will them-selves become tricky. If those who are in office indulge in covetousness [avidity], which differs little from appro-priation by robbery, then the people will be in a miserable state and will not be stabilized. All these faults, however, are not due to the nature of the people but to the avidity and cruelty of the rulers that have perverted the nature of the people. No sooner do the causes of trouble begin with those in high posts than the people below act under the influence of their superiors and imitate them. This is ac-complished without the people's awareness. Hence, it is charged that "The things that people practice are not good." That we are to blame the people on this ground is very perplexing.

The *Greater Odes* of the *Book of Poetry* says:

> Get water from a remote brook of the wayside. Draw it in
> one container and pour it into another. Then it may be used
> to steam rice and to prepare a feast. A gentle and happy ruler
> should be parent of the people in some similar way.[47]

This means that if the superior man attains a virtuous nature, he is a gift to his people because he will do good for
them. The *Greater Odes* says again:

> By the wayside, there lay reeds in thickness. Don't let cows
> and sheep step upon them. Very soon they will flower, and
> very soon they will grow tall. They will have soft and juicy
> leaves.[48]

This depicts the superior men endowed with the virtue of
benevolence.

Appendix: Romanization and Corresponding Chinese Characters

An Hui Ts'ung Shu 安徽叢書
An-hui 安徽

ch'ang 常
Chang Tsai 張載
chêng 貞
chêng 徵
ch'êng 誠
Ch'êng Hao 程灝
Chêng-mêng 正蒙
Ch'êng-shih yi-shu 程氏遺書
Ch'êng Yi 程頤
ch'i 氣
ch'i-chih 氣質
ch'i-chih-chih-hsing 氣質之性
Ch'i-ching shiao-chi 七經小記
ch'i-ping 氣稟
chia-shu 家塾
Chiang Yung 江永
ch'iao 巧
chiao 教
"*Chieh-pi*" 解蔽
chien 簡
ch'ien 乾
ch'ien-kua 乾卦
chih 知
chih 智
chih 直
Ch'in 秦
Ch'ing 清
ch'ing 情

ching 靜
ching 經
"*Ching Hsin*" 盡心下
ch'ing-miao 清廟
Chung-kuo ching-shih ssŭ-hsiang shiao-shih 中國近世思想小史
Chou Tun-yi 周敦頤
Chou Yü 周語
ch'ü-ch'i-wei, pu-pao-ch'i-shih 去其畏, 不暴其使
"*Ch'ü-hsia*" 胠篋
Chu Hsi 朱熹
chü jên 舉人
Chuan 傳
chüan 卷
ch'üan 權
Chuang Chou 莊周
Chuang Tzŭ 莊子
chüeh 覺
Ch'un Ch'iu 春秋
chün-tzŭ 君子
chung 忠
chung 中
chung-ho 中和
Chung Yung 中庸

êrh shun 耳順
Êrh Ya 爾雅

Fa-hsiang lun 法象論
fang ch'i liang-hsin 放其良心

fei-ch'i-shu-hsi-yü-yi-chê-yeh 非其素習於儀者也
fên 分
fu-ch'i chih-ling 附氣之靈
fu-hsing chih-ling 附形之靈
fu-ming 復命
Fung Yu-lan 馮友蘭

hai-tao 害道
Han Yü 韓愈
hêng 亨
ho 合
ho 和
huo-jan 豁然
ho-p'i-chih-chi 闔闢之機
Hou Wai-lu 侯外廬
Hsi Tzŭ Ta Chuan 繫辭大傳
hsiang 庠
hsiang 祥
"*Hsiang yin-chiu yi*" 鄉飲酒義
hsin 心
hsin 信
hsin-chih-suo-t'ung-jan 心之所同然
hsin-chih 心知
Hsin li-hsüeh 新理學
hsing 性
"*Hsing O*" 性惡
hsing-shan 性善
hsiu 秀
hsiu-ch'i 秀氣
hsin-chih 心知
Hsiu Ning 休寧
hsü 序
Hsü Chieh 徐鍇
Hsü Shên 許慎
Hsü Yen 緒言
hsüeh 血
hsüeh 學
hsüeh-ch'i 血氣
hsüeh-ch'i hsin-chih 血氣心知

Hsün Tzŭ 荀子
Hu Shih 胡適
hua 化
hua-chih-liu 化之流
Huang Tsung-hsi 黃宗羲
hun 魂
hun-p'o 魂魄
Hung Fan 洪範
huo yü tê 惑於德

jên 任
jên 仁
jên-lun 人倫
jên-tao 人道

kan 感
K'ao-kung-chi-t'u chu 攷工記圖注
Kao T'ao Mo 皋陶謨
Kao Tzŭ 告子
kê wu 格物
k'o-chieh-chih shih-yü-shê-yeh 可詰之使語塞也
"*Ku-ching-chieh kou-ch'ên hsü*" 古經解鉤沉序
Ku Yen-wu 顧炎武
Kuan Tzŭ 管子
"*Kuang-Ya*" 廣雅
kuei 鬼
kuei-shên 鬼神
k'un 坤
K'un-kua 坤卦
"*K'un wen-yen*" 坤文言
k'ung 空
K'ung Tzŭ 孔子
Kuo Yü 國語

Lao Tan 老聃
li 禮
li 理

Li Chi 禮記
li-chieh 理解
li-jên chih-tao 立人之道
Li Wei
li-yi 理義
li-yi 禮義
ling 靈
Liu Hsia-hui 柳下惠
Li Yün 禮運
Lu Chiu-yüan 陸九淵
Lü Shih Ch'un Ch'iu 呂氏春秋
Lun Hêng 論衡
Lun Yü 論語

mei 美
Mêng Tzŭ tzŭ-yi shu-chêng
　孟子字義疏證
Ming-Ju hsüeh-an 明儒學案
Mo Ti 墨翟

nêng 能

o 我
o, oh 惡

P'an-kêng 盤庚
Pei Hu T'ung 白虎通
Po Yi 伯夷
pên-jan chih-tê 本然之德
Pên-ming 本命
p'i 否
pi 悖
pi 蔽
pi-jan 必然
pieh 別
p'ien 偏
p'o 魄
pu-jên 不仁

pu-hsin 不信
pu-shan 不善
pu-yi 不義

san-kang 三綱
shan 善
shang-ti 上帝
Shao Yung 邵雍
shên 神
shên-ming 神明
shêng 聖
shêng-jên 聖人
shêng-shêng 生生
shih 實
shih 事
shih 時
shih 師
Shih Ching 詩經
Shih-hsün 釋訓
"*Shih-ku*" 釋詁
Ssŭ Shu 四書
shu 塾
su 素
Shu Ching 書經
Shu Ching Yu Kung 書經禹貢
shu 恕
shun 順
Shuo Wen 說文
Shuo Wen hsi-chuan 說文繫傳
ssŭ 私
shih 師
shih ch'i pên-hsin 失其本心
Ssŭ K'u Ch'uan Shu Kuan
　四庫全書館
Ssŭ-shih 四時
sung 頌
Sung-kao 崧高

ta-ch'ing-ming 大清明
ta êrh hua chih wei chih shêng
　大而化之謂之聖

Ta Hsüeh 大學
ta-kung 大公
ta-kung 大共
Ta P'êng chin-shih Yün-ch'u shu
答彭進士允初書
Ta Tai Li Chi 大戴禮記
Ta Ya 大雅
Tai Chên 戴震
Tai-shih yi-shu 戴氏遺書
Tai Tung-yüan Chi 戴東原集
*Tai Tung-yüan êrh-pai-nien
shêng-jih chi-nien lun-wen chi*
戴東原二百年生日記念論文集
*Tai Tung-yüan hsien-shêng
nien-p'u* 戴東原先生年譜
Tai Tung-yüan tê-chê-hsüeh
戴東原的哲學
tao 道
Tao Te Ching 道德經
tao-yi 道義
tê 德
tê 得
Tê Ch'ung Fu 德充符
t'iao-li 條理
t'ien-ming wei-hsing 天命維新
t'ien-tao 天道
t'ien-tê 天德
t'ien-tê chih-chih 天德之知
t'ien-ti 天地
t'ien-ti chih hsing 天地之性
ting 定
ts'ai 才
ts'ai chih 才質
tsang shih 藏識
Tsêng Tzŭ 曾子
Tso Chuan 左傳
Tsou Yen 鄒衍
T'so Ch'ao Ch'i-nien Chuan-shu
左昭七年傳疏
Tu Mêng-tzŭ lun-hsing
讀孟子論性

Tu Yi Hsi-tz'ŭ lun-hsing
讀易繫辭論性
tui-ou 對偶
t'ung 通
Tung Chung-shu 董仲舒
Tuan Yü-ts'ai 段玉裁
tzŭ 字
Tzŭ Ch'an 子產
Tzŭ Chang 子張
tzŭ-jan 自然

Wang Fu-chih 王夫之
Wang Yang-ming 王陽明
wu-ch'ang 五常
wu-hsing 五行
wu-lun 五倫
Wu-yi 無逸
wu-yü 無慾

yang 陽
yang 羊
Yang Chu 楊朱
Yeh-hu-ch'an 野狐禪
Yen Yüan 顏元
yi 義
yi-chih tsê yü-ch'in 易知則有親
yi-chien 意見
Yi Ching 易經
yi li-chih hsing 義理之性
yin 陰
yin-shên 陰神
yin-yang 陰陽
yin yang pu ts'ê chih wei shên
陰陽不測之謂神
yü 欲
yü 玉
Yü 禹
yu ch'in 有親
Yü Hsia Shu 虞夏書
"*Yü mou shu*" 與某書

"*Yu Shih Lan, Ming Lei*"
　有始覽名類
yüan 原
yüan 元
Yüan Ch'ên 原臣
Yüan Chün 原君
Yüan Fa 原法

Yüan Jên 原人
Yüan Shan 原善
Yüan Tao 原道
Yüeh-ch'i 樂記
Yüeh-ling 月令
Yüeh-ling 樂林
yung 勇

Notes

INTRODUCTION

1. In the collections of writings on Confucianism such as *The Confucian Persuasion* (Stanford, 1960); *Confucian in Action,* edited by David Nivison and Arthur Wright; and *Confucian Personalities* (Stanford, 1962), edited by Arthur Wright; we find excellent discussions of Confucianism as an ideology and institutional practice but little discussions of Confucianism as a system of ethical and metaphysical ideas. Joseph Levenson's *Confucian China and Its Modern Fate,* vol. 1 (Berkeley, 1958), an example of the historical type, pays attention only to the historical explanation and, sometimes, to a psychological reduction (which Levenson calls "emotional commitment to tradition") of the Confucian thought. The genuine Confucian philosophy of many significant modern Confucian scholar-thinkers is bypassed or completely explained away.

2. This *li* is different from the *li* for propriety or the *li* for advantage. In the rest of the paper I shall use the term *"li"* only to stand for the notion of principle or reason.

3. In the sense that it can be interpreted either as observing or examining things in nature for the purpose of finding their principles *(li)* of existence, as Wang Yang-ming apparently understood what Chu Hsi held, or as rectifying the intentions of the mind, as Wang Yang-ming himself proposed.

4. *"Pi"* has been translated by Burton Watson as "obsession" in his translation of Hsün Tzŭ's writings, *Hsün Tzŭ: Basic Writings* (New York: Columbia University Press, 1963), pp. 12–18. I prefer "beclouding" in translating *"pi"* because *"pi"* generally refers to the eclipsing of the light from the light source. In this context, *"pi"* refers to the eclipsing of

4. *(Continued)*

the light of reason or what Descartes would have called "the natural light."

5. Here "rational vision" is intended to refer to the natural insights of mind when mind is not obstructed or shadowed by prejudices and desires or emotions. I use the term in an effort to distinguish the activities of the mind *(hsin)* from the mind itself. It seems to me that "beclouding" is related to the former, rather than to the latter.

6. In the later development of the Wang Yang-ming school, its followers who claimed to embrace truth through direct insight and sudden enlightenment of mind tended toward extreme naturalism and made it an excuse for unconventional behavior and undisciplined conduct. Cf. Huang Tsung-hsi's discussion of the T'ai-chou school in *Ming-Ju hsüeh-an* [Philosophical Records of Ming Confucian Scholars]. For a short description, see Carsun Chang's *The Development of Neo-Confucian Thought,* vol. 2 (New York: Bookman Associates, 1962), pp. 113–41.

7. Cf. comments and translations of Wang Fu-chih and Yen Yüan in Wing-tsit Chan's *A Source Book in Chinese Philosophy*, pp. 692, 708.

8. Cf. Hu Shih's *Tai Tung-yüan tê-chê-hsüeh* [Philosophy of Tai Tung-yüan], chapter 2, section 1.

9. Here my description of Tai Chên's life is a brief one. A fuller description of his life can be found in: Arthur W. Hummel, ed., *Eminent Chinese of the Ch'ing Period* (1644–1912), vol. 2 (New York: Pergamon Press, 1944), pp. 695–700. My emphasis here is on his philosophical writings.

10. Since then until his death, he has contributed to the editing of the Ssŭ K'u Series of books.

11. This work later was incorporated into the series of books called *Ch'i-ching shiao-chi* [Small Records of Seven Classics].

12. For the discussion of these writings, see Hu Shih's *Philosophy of Tai Tung-yüan.*

13. I have translated into English in this book the *Yüan Shan* [Inquiry into Goodness], with explanatory notes. No other translation in Western languages has yet been made.

14. See Tuan Yü-ts'ai, *"Tai Tung-yüan hsien-shêng nien-p'u"* [Biographical Chronology of Tai Tung-yüan]; reprinted in the *Tai Tung-yüan Chi* [Collections of Essays of Tai Tung-yüan], part 2, pp. 84–120.

15. Wing-tsit Chan has translated part of this work in his *A Source Book in Chinese Philosophy,* pp. 711–22.

16. See note 14, Introduction.

17. Two reasons have been given for this: First, the *Inquiry into Goodness* is a systematic work, and it develops Tai Chên's own thought on cosmology and ethics independently of references to earlier Classics (as we must note that the reference part of the *Inquiry into Goodness* was a later addition). Second, this short work is as comprehensive as, but perhaps more cogent than, his later work concerning the *Mêng Tzŭ* [Book of Mencius], namely, *Commentaries on the Meanings of Terms in the* Book of Mencius.

18. See Tai Chên, *Mêng Tzŭ tzŭ-yi shu-chêng* [Commentaries on the Meanings of Terms in the *Book of Mencius*], section on *li.*

19. In the volume on the Ch'ing and Modern periods in the *Anthology of Philosophical Essays,* compiled by the Institute of Philosophy at the Chinese Academy of Sciences, 1961, the editors compare Tai Chên's notion of *li* and Han Fei Tzŭ's explanation of *li* in terms of the characteristics of concrete things such as lightness and heaviness, whiteness and blackness, and smallness and largeness. According to Han Fei Tzŭ in his essay that explains Lao Tzŭ's doctrine, once the *li* in things are determined or ascertained, we can easily divide things and speak about things.

20. See Tai Chên, *Commentaries on the Meanings of Terms in the* Book of Mencius, section on *li.*

21. See Tai Chên, "Letter to Tuan Yü-ts'ai" in: the *Biographical Chronology of Tai Tung-yüan.*

22. *Ibid.*

23. See the *Book of Mencius,* chapter 6, concerning Mencius' discourse on human nature.

24. Tai Chên, *Commentaries on the Meanings of Terms in the* Book of Mencius, section on *li.*

25. Tai Chên, *Commentaries on the Meanings of Terms in the* Book of Mencius, section on *li* and section on *jên, yi, li,* and *choh.*

26. See Hu Shih, *Philosophy of Tai Tung-yüan,* pp. 62–63 ff.

27. Chou Tun-yi and Ch'êng Hao speak of tranquility *(ching)* or desirelessness *(ting)* as the ideal goal of a righteous life in accordance with the Way. Ch'êng Yi and Chu Hsi speak extensively on the subject of preserving reverence or seriousness *(ching* or *ch'êng)* as a way at arriving at virtue and truth.

28. This reference is to Chou Tun-yi's doctrine regarding how to cultivate the way of the sages. Cf. his *T'ung-shu* [Book of Penetrating Comprehension in Regard to the *Book of Changes*], parts of which have been translated by Wing-tsit Chan and which appear in Chan's *A Source Book in Chinese Philosophy,* pp. 460–80.

29. See Tai Chên, *Commentaries on the Meanings of Terms in the* Book of Mencius, section on *li.*

30. Or prudence. See Tai Chên, *Commentaries on the Meanings of Terms in the* Book of Mencius, section on *ch'üan.*

31. It is Tai Chên's suspicion that the Neo-Confucianists, who talk about *li* have identified *li* with the *alaya (tsang-shih)* in Buddhism. See Tai Chên, *Commentaries on the Meanings of Terms in the* Book of Mencius, section on *ch'üan.*

32. Cf. Chang Tsai's *Chêng-Mêng* [Rectifying Youthful Ignorance].

33. Cf. *Ch'êng-shih yi-shu* [Remaining Writings of the Ch'êng Brothers], parts 18, 21, 25.

34. We may point out also that whereas Mencius talks of having only few desires, the Neo-Confucianists talk of having no desires.

35. This is a literal saying of Tai Chên; see his *Yu-P'êng Chin-shih Yün-ch'u shu* [Letter to Chin-shih P'êng].

36. The last two essays were later incorporated into Tai Chên's *Inquiry into Goodness.*

37. See Tai Chên, *Commentaries on the Meanings of Terms in the Book of Mencius,* section on *t'ien-tao* (the Heavenly Way).

38. Tai Chên, *Fa-hsiang lun* [On Law and Phenomena].

39. Tai Chên, *Tu Yi Hsi-tz'ŭ lun-hsing* [Reading the *Great Appendixes* on Nature in the *Book of Changes*]. See also the opening sentence of the *Inquiry into Goodness.*

40. I have argued that it is Mencius who first contrasted *hsing* with *ming* in order to argue for the goodness of human nature. I also pointed out that *hsing* represents the freedom or the free will of man, whereas *ming* represents the given conditions of life; hence, my translation of *ming* as "necessity." See my monograph, *"Chan-kuo yü-chia tê ssŭ-hsiang chi ch'i fa chan"* [Thoughts of the Confucianists in the Period of Warring States and Their Development], sponsored by the Academia Sinica, Taipei, for the *History of Ancient China,* in the *Bulletin of the Institute of History and Philology,* Academia Sinica, vol. 40, 1968, pp. 881–912.

41. See Tai Chên, *Inquiry into Goodness,* chapter 3.

42. See Tai Chên, *Inquiry into Goodness,* chapter 2.

43. These three virtues are fundamental virtues in Tai Chên's *Inquiry into Goodness.* For more explanations besides this introduction, see explanatory notes to chapter 1 of my translation of the *Inquiry into Goodness.*

44. See the *Lun Yü* [Analects] and the *Chung Yung* [Doctrine of the Mean].

45. This is the main point of Tai Chên's *Inquiry into Goodness.*

46. See Tai Chên, *Inquiry into Goodness,* chapter 3.

47. Tai Chên, *Commentaries on the Meanings of Terms in the Book of Mencius,* section on *tao.*

48. The well-known American idealist philosopher Josiah Royce has pointed out that there is always a discrepancy between the religious and the moral, as the former is intended for

48. *(Continued)*

    ultimate salvation and the latter is intended for mundane happiness.

49. That is, evil is defined as the privation of good. This line of thought has also received considerations in the Western philosophy. Leibniz and Spinoza, for example, are spokesmen for this view.

50. That human nature does not participate in a priori evil and that evilness results from the contact of human nature with external circumstances are further testified to in the *Li Chi* [Record of Rites] by the notion of human nature as being originally pure but susceptible to circumstantial influences toward evil or goodness.

51. Cf. the essay concerning *"Chieh Pi"* [Removing Becloudings] and that concerning *"Hsing O"* [Man's Nature Is Evil] in the *Writings of Hsün Tzŭ*. Translations are available in Burton Watson, trans., *Hsün Tzŭ: Basic Writings*.

52. See Tai Chên, *Commentaries on the Meanings of Terms in the Book of Mencius,* section on *ts'ai.*

53. That is, in the sense of the *Analects* and the *Ta Hsüeh* [Great Learning].

54. See Tuan Yü-ts'ai, *Biographical Chronology of Tai Tung-yüan.*

55. *Ibid.*

56. Tai Chên, *"Ku-ching-chieh kou-ch'en hsü"* [Preface to Someone's Fishing the Sunken in Explanation of the Ancient Classics], *Collection of Essays of Tai Tung-yüan,* part 2, pp. 35–36.

57. Cf. also Tai Chên, *"Yü mou shu"* [Open Letter to Someone], *Collection of Essays of Tai Tun-yuan,* part 2, pp. 32–33.

TAI CHÊN'S PREFACE

1. The Chinese title *Yüan Shan* means "on the meaning and origin of the conception of *shan,* which is goodness." It is customary for Chinese scholars to write a systematic explanation of some important notion or principle and give it a title beginning

1. *(Continued)*

    with the character *"yüan."* For example, Han Yü wrote his *Yüan Tao* [Inquiry into the Way] and the *Yüan Jên* [Inquiry into Man]. Huang Chung-hsi wrote his *Yüan Chun* [Inquiry into the Notion of Ruler], the *Yüan Ch'ên* [Inquiry into the Notion of Subjects], and the *Yüan Fa* [Inquiry into the Notion of Law].

2. The term "Confucian Classics" here refers to the five Confucian Classics: the *Yi Ching* [Book of Changes], the *Shu Ching* [Book of Documents], the *Li Chi* [Record of Rites], the *Shih Ching* [Book of Poetry], the *Ch'un Ch'iu* [Spring and Autumn Annals]; and the four Confucian books, the *Lun Yü* [Analects], the *Mêng Tzŭ* [Book of Mencius], the *Chung Yung* [Doctrine of the Mean], and the *Ta Hsüeh* [Great Learning]. The five Classics are recognized as the bases of Confucianism by the Han Confucianists. The *Ssŭ Shu* [Four Books] were first singled out as introductory documents for teaching Confucianism by Chu Hsi (1130–1200 A.D.), a great Sung Neo-Confucianist.

3. "The Way of Heaven" *(t'ien-tao)* refers to the ultimate reality and norm of things in the world. Both *"t'ien"* and *"tao"* are used in the earliest Confucian Classics such as the *Book of Documents*, the *Book of Poetry*, and the *Record of Rites*. The term *"t'ien"* refers to Heaven, the willful, but not necessarily personalistic, supreme authority in the universe; *"tao"* refers to the way that things should follow or cultivate. Later the notions of *tao* or *t'ien*, or *t'ien-tao*, are used very much in the text by Tai Chen. They are also explained in terms of the doctrine of the complementary activities of the masculine *(yang)* and the feminine *(yin)* forces. Hereafter, I shall capitalize the words "Heaven" or "the Way" or "the Way of Heaven" when they are used to refer to the Confucian notions of *t'ien*, *tao*, or *t'ien-tao*.

4. "The Way of Man" *(jên-tao)* refers to the right way or norm that a man should naturally adopt and follow in self-cultivation and self-realization. It is also a Confucian notion closely related to, and should naturally be congenial with, the Way of Heaven. The *Book of Changes* speaks of "establishing the Way of Man" *(li-jên chih-tao)*. (This phrase can also be understood as "the way of establishing the man." But given

4. *(Continued)*

the above notion of *jên-tao*, the first rendering seems to be the correct and natural one.) We may even say that the Way of Man is the exhibition of the Way of Heaven in the special case of man. It is further a realization or a potentiality for the realization of the Way of Heaven. As we shall see, Tai Chên sometimes identifies the Way of Man with the natural and with the good nature of man and man's potentiality for the full development of goodness.

5. The term *"chia-shu"* may also refer to the family school or some side hall in the house of the author. According to the *Êrh-Ya*, a hall on the side of a house gate is referred to as *shu*. It is said in chapter 18 in the *Record of Rites* that "In ancient times, a community will have a *hsiang* for teaching; a family will have a *shu* for teaching."

CHAPTER 1

1. The term *"shan"* (goodness) appears in the *Lun Yü* [Analects], the *Chung Yung* [Doctrine of the Mean], the *Li Chi* [Record of Rites], the *Yi Ching* [Book of Changes], and other Classical philosophical writings. It has the general meaning of good or goodness. Hsü Shên (d. 120 A.D.) in his *Shuo Wen* [On Words] explains it as meaning the same as *"yi"* (righteousness) and as *"mei"* (beauty). All the three words are related to the word *"yang"* (lamb), which stands for a sacrifice bringing good luck and which therefore gives rise to the word *"hsiang,"* which means good omen or good luck. It starts with Mencius that *shan* is applied to the nature of man to the effect that all men are considered originally and equally good in their nature and that they can develop and perform moral virtues. This means that *shan* is the basis and the origin of virtues. Tai Chên evidently continues this line of thought. Another point to be noted is that *shan* need not be used as a noun with the denotation of good or goodness. It can be used as an adjective meaning "skilled in" and as a verb meaning "to benefit." Both of these uses are found in the *Mêng Tzǔ* [Book of Mencius].

2. The term *"jên"* has been translated variously as "human-hearted," "humanity," "complete virtue," "goodness," "humaneness," "benevolence," and so on. The translation

2. *(Continued)*

here is intended to be very general. The specific connotation of the term as used by Tai Chên will be found later in the discussion. For Confucius, *jên* is related to both *"chung"* (loyalty) and *"shu"* (compassion). The term *"chung"* refers to a personal commitment to goodness and therefore loyalty to an ideal of oneself that consists in developing oneself into perfection as much as one can; *"shu"* is the capacity to think of other men's needs in terms of one's own and hence an effort to help others to attain their moral perfection and well-being. In the Neo-Confucian tradition, *jên* is considered not only the prototype of all virtues but also the fundamental metaphysical power of the formation and transformation of the Way. Hence, *jên* becomes a metaphysical as well as a moral principle. As a metaphysical principle, it is a principle of synthetic unity and comprehensive creativity of life.

3. The term *"li"* refers to the rules of conduct governing human relationships such as those of ruler to subjects, father to son, wife to husband, older brother to younger brother, and friend to friend. In its earlier use in the *Record of Rites* and the *Analects*, it may indeed denotatively refer to some specifiable rituals or ceremonies governing these human relationships. According to *On Words*, *li* were originally rites performed to serve gods and to secure benediction. But one must not take *li* to be merely empty forms of ritual conduct; the *Record of Rites* speaks of *li* as the unchangeable principles of reason (chapter 19) and as the concrete fruits of righteousness (chapter 9). In chapters 10 and 30, *li* is considered by the author of the *Record of Rites* as arising from the restraints and refinements of human conduct in accordance with the feelings of man that conform to the natural and social demands. In the *Analects*, *li* is regarded as the embodiment of *jên* and as a necessary form for the substantial development of virtues.

4. The term *"yi,"* like *"jên"* and *"li,"* is used in its broad sense; namely, the sense of being right and good. *On Words* indicates that *"yi"* is etymologically associated with *"hsiang"* (good) and *"o"* (I). It is therefore the dignified air of a person. In this regard, one might remotely compare *yi* with Kant's notion of respect for the dignity of man, or the respect for a person as an end (the ideal humanity). However, in the

4. *(Continued)*

    Doctrine of the Mean, *yi* is defined as what is appropriate and proper. In chapter 24 of the *Record of Rites*, *yi* is said to be what is proper for a *given* situation. In chapter 32 of the *Record of Rites*, *tao* is itself said to be *yi*, meaning, according to the commentary, that *yi* is the principle according to which things are judged to be right or wrong. For Classical Confucianists, particularly for Mencius, *yi* is contrasted with *li* (profit). *Yi* is therefore the ground of the human act that is not directed toward self-love or self-interest but instead is aimed at preserving the intrinsic appropriateness of the act. Indeed, *yi*, besides being a principle of righteousness, can be considered, for Tai Chên, an innate capacity of man to do the right things or to follow righteousness, because, as we have seen, *yi* is one of the three main given goodnesses—*yi*, *jên*, *li*—in the nature of Heaven and in the nature of man. Furthermore, *yi* also has its metaphysical meaning. It refers to the very nature of Heaven and Earth that causes the creation of things according to the patterns of reason. It is, in this sense, metaphysically connotative. To know *yi* is to know precisely the patterning and ordering of things in the process of the creative activity of the Way. Apparently, it is owing to this metaphysical feature of *yi* that a man may decide to follow a principle of reason and justify his actions by it. It is meant for realizing a quality of man that preserves, and conduces to the preservation of, the ordering and harmony of things in the world.

5. *On Words* interprets the verb *"shun"* as meaning "accords with a pattern." The noun *"shun"* therefore connotes conformity or accordance with a pattern, a principle, or reason. In the *Chou Li* (Rites of Chou), the direction from up to down is called *shun*. *Shun* as a virtue is suggested in the *Analects* where Confucius speaks of being *êrh shun* at sixty: "My ears find no obstruction in accepting the world when I was sixty." Mencius speaks of *shun* in connection with one's attitude towards his parents. Hsün Tzŭ speaks of *shun* as consisting in living harmoniously with others through goodness. Perhaps, *shun* can simply mean goodness, for in the *Shih Ching* [Book of Poetry], *shun* is used contrastively with *"p'i"* (badness or misfortune). In this sense, *shun* is virtually the same as harmony and concordance.

6. *On Words* explains *"hsin"* as *"ch'êng"* (sincerity), which, of course, can be regarded as being closely related to the virtue of truthfulness or trustworthiness. But here in Tai Chên's usage, it need not be interpreted merely as a moral virtue of man. The term *"hsin,"* like *"ch'êng,"* has its metaphysical connotation in its suggesting an intrinsic quality of Heaven, which manifests itself in the reality (Way) of the ten thousand things.

7. The term *"ch'ang"* refers to the basic constant structure or order of things and human relationships. For example, the *Book of Changes* in its *"K'un-kua"* speaks of *ch'ang* as constancy, and Lao Tzŭ speaks of it as the constant reversion of things *(fu-ming)*. The so-called *wu-ch'ang* or *wu-lun* refers to the following human relationship: the relation between ruler and the subjects, the relation between father and son, the relation between husband and wife, the relation between older brother and younger brother, and, finally, the relation between friend and friend. These five relationships have been first mentioned in the *Book of Mencius* and the *Doctrine of the Mean*. They are considered as embodying claims upon man for developing virtues accordingly. The metaphysical and ethical philosophies of Confucianism are realistic, because they are based on a recognition of the natural as well as the moral order of things and men as being both objective and stable. It should be noted that Wang Ch'ung in his book *Lun Hêng* [Discourses and Evaluations] refers to *"wu-ch'ang"* as the following virtues: *jên, yi, li, chih,* and *hsin*. This seems to overlap with what Tai Chên takes to be the qualities of goodness and the virtues of Heaven.

8. The term *"hua"* means change or transformation and is used philosophically in the *Book of Changes* to refer to both empirically observable and empirically unobservable subtleties of bringing about or issuing forth things; hence, the creative and productive change and process of the formation and transformation. It carries an implication of continuity and smoothness. The *hua* of Heaven and Earth has two aspects—the dynamic (life) and the static (quiescence)—that correspond to the *yin-yang* movements of the Way, as the Way is manifested in nothing but the *hua* of Heaven and Earth. *Hua* therefore is essentially different from a causal change; it is

8. *(Continued)*

also different from the change spoken in terms of a creation or destruction by divine providence, as it is in the Christian religion.

9. The *Doctrine of the Mean* says that what Heaven ordains is *hsing*, or nature. The Confucianists believe that nature is what is given in existence and in value. Confucius speaks of the *hsing* of man as being closely similar. Mencius considers the *hsing* of man to be basically good. For Mencius, what is given in a man as *hsing* is good and is a basis for developing virtues. It is this conception of *hsing* that Tai Chên wants to define and explain in his *Yüan Shan* [Inquiry into Goodness] and in his earlier work, the *Mêng Tzŭ tzŭ-yi shu-chêng* [Commentaries of the Meanings of Terms in the *Book of Mencius*].

10. The terms "heaven" *(t'ien)* and "earth" *(ti)* are used in the Confucian Classics (in the *Shu Ching* [Book of Documents] and in the *Shi Ching* [*Book of Poetry*]) to refer to the principal manifestations of the Way. The term *"t'ien-ti"* or *"t'ien"* is very often used in such a way that *t'ien* can be substituted for the Way. The *Book of Changes* suggests the doctrine that the interchange of the *yin* and *yang* is called the Way; that is, *t'ien* and *ti* are the concrete illustrations of the complementary operation of the masculine and feminine forces of the Way. As such, they are conceived of as having a virtue of benevolence or creativity *(jên)*.

11. The term *"ming"* occurs as early as in the *Book of Documents* and in the *Book of Poetry*. In the *Book of Documents*, *ming* is the dictate of *t'ien* (Heaven) or the *shang-ti* (lord on the high). While *ming* is a dictate of *t'ien* or *ti* in many odes in the *Book of Poetry*, in others in the same work, *ming* is the same thing as the Way. One ode *(sung, ch'ing-miao)* reads: *"t'ien-ming wei-hsing"* (The will *(ming)* of Heaven never ceases to function and operate). It is the Way conceived of as a force with an internal necessity and authority that prescribes its own destiny and course of activity. But the Way is at the same time totally natural, totally spontaneous, totally creative, and full of potentiality. In this sense the Way gives rise to *tê* (virtue) and *hsing* (nature). Hence, *ming* and *hsing* may refer to the same existent thing, but *hsing* constitutes the potentiality for development and

11. *(Continued)*

growth in the existent thing, whereas *ming* provides the limitations and restrictions of the development of the thing and the necessity of its present constitution. See also note 9, chapter 1.

12. According to the *Shuo Wen Hsi-chuan* [Appended Commentary Concerning *On Words*] by Hsü Chieh (920–974 A.D.), "*hsiu*" is the fruit of a growing grain. It refers to the refined part of anything. Thus, in the *Record of Rites*, we have the saying that "Man is the *hsiu-ch'i* (the refined vital force) of the five agencies," which are metal, wood, water, fire, and earth.

13. The term "*ts'ai*" refers to the raw material from which things are made. But it also refers to the ability or capacity of a living being as permitted by natural endowment; it differs, therefore, from "*nêng*" in that the latter refers to capacities or capabilities—both natural and acquired. See also note 14, chapter 1.

14. The term "*nêng*" is the natural or acquired capacity or capability of a living being. It is often used together with "*ts'ai*," which refers principally to natural capabilities. See note 13, chapter 1.

15. The terms "*hsüeh*" (blood) and "*ch'i*" (breath) here refer to the physical nature of desires and feelings; "*hsin*" (mind) and "*chih*" (intelligence), on the other hand, refer to the higher mental faculties of man. The compound term "*hsüeh-ch'i hsin-chih*" was first used in the chapter titled "*Yüeh-ch'i*" [Record of Music] in the *Record of Rites:* "People have the nature of *hsüeh-ch'i hsin-chih* but do not have constant sorrow, joy, delight, and anger."

16. The signs *(chêng)* of the natural refer to the products of nature and the process of the formation and transformation of Heaven and Earth.

17. The virtue of supreme illumination or supreme intelligence *(shên-ming)* refers to the spirit-like process of the formation and transformation of Heaven and Earth. It can also be described as a state of supreme illumination through which a man will know and participate in the creative as well as the

17. *(Continued)*

preserving activities of Heaven and Earth. Thus, the *Hsi Tzŭ* [Great Appendixes], part 1, of the *Book of Changes* speaks of "being divine and illuminating the world." One might also say that *shên-ming* consists in the clarity and penetrating power of one's mind when its capacity is fully cultivated. In this regard, it is similar to Hsün Tzu's idea of *ta-ch'ing-ming* (great, clear illumination) in his essay *"Chieh-pi"* [On Removing Becloudings]. See also note 17, chapter 2; note 4, chapter 3.

18. The word *"chih"* (opinion or knowledge) has the same pronunciation and tone as the word *"chih"* (wisdom or prudence). But there is a difference between these two: *chih* (wisdom or prudence) refers to an understanding of the nature of things and men that will warrant good action. In the *Kuan Tzŭ Ssŭ Shih* [On the Four Seasons by Kuan Tzŭ], it is said that "knowing" one thing and "knowing" how to vary is *chih* (wisdom or prudence). *Chih* (wisdom or prudence) is thus wisdom or practical wisdom or sagacity. *Chih* (opinion or knowledge), as used in the *Book of Documents*, the *Book of Changes*, the *Analects*, and the *Record of Rites*, on the other hand, refers to knowledge or knowing in general and sometimes to the subjective beliefs of a man.

19. The term *"ch'üan"* etymologically means "weight," as given in the *Kuo Yü*, the *Chou Yü* [Record of Chou], the *"Shih-ku"* [An Explanation of *"Ku"*] in the *Kuang Ya*, and the *"Ch'ü-hsia"* [Opening Boxes] in the *Chuang Tzŭ* [Writings by Chuang Chou]; hence, to weigh, to exercise discretion, to change from the *ching*, or the regular, according to circumstances. The regular is the Way *(tao)*. But *ch'üan* is the regulation of the irregular in accordance with *ching*. Thus, Mencius says: "To give your sister-in-law a helping hand when she is drowning is *ch'üan*" (*Book of Mencius*, 4A, 18). *Ch'üan* is used in the same sense in the *Record of Rites* (chapters 4 and 39). The term *"ch'üan"* can therefore be considered a principle of application; it is a norm prescribing the following of norms in different circumstances. Hence, it is a virtue that involves one's capacity of making careful evaluation of things and mature judgment. We may perhaps suggest that it is the actual application of *chih* (wisdom or prudence).

20. The term *"tao"* is a common word in the Classical Chinese philosophy of Taoism and Confucianism. It refers to the ultimate reality or the truth or the principle of existence and development. To say that goodness is *tao* is to say that the nature of *tao* is good, self-sufficient, and self-justifiable.

21. The word *"tê"* first occurs in the *Book of Poetry*, the *Book of Documents*, and the *Book of Changes*. According to the section concerning *"ku"* in the *Kuang Ya* in the *Êrh Ya*, *"tê"* means *"tê"* (gain). Chuang Tzŭ speaks of *"tê"* as what a living thing obtains in order to live *(t'ien-ti)*, as what an event obtains in order to become what it is, and as what a thing obtains to achieve harmony *(Tê-ch'ung-fu)*. A metaphysical explanation comes from the *Book of Changes:* "The interaction and communication of the *yin* and *yang* is called *tê.*" In the *Analects*, *tê* refers to the capacity for virtue endowed in a man and to the actual virtue as resulting from cultivating that capacity in man. It is therefore something, again, objective and natural. In the *Tao Tê Ching* [Book of Lao Tzŭ *or* The Way and Its Power] of Lao Tzŭ, *tê* refers to the inner potential qualities of the Way and things. It is justifiably identified therefore with virtue and with the power of virtue.

22. The term *"ch'êng"* is in its ethical sense the virtue of sincerity. But in its metaphysical sense, it refers to what is real and true. The *Doctrine of the Mean* says: *"Ch'êng* is the Way of Heaven, and to realize and fulfill *ch'êng* is the Way of Man."* That Heaven is creative and productive implies that *ch'êng* as a virtue of Heaven is creativity. A man who preserves or develops this virtue would thus make himself creative and productive. The quotation from the *Doctrine of the Mean* also testifies that, in the Confucian philosophy, man is not separated from Heaven and that he has a unique significance in the scheme of things because it is only man who can achieve and fulfill the virtue of Heaven.

23. Etymologically, *"t'iao"* means "twig" or "tree," according to *Shuo Wen;* and "longish," according to *"Yu-kung"* in the *Book of Documents*. In the *"P'an-kêng"* of the *Book of Documents*, it is used in the sense of "following into order." The term *"li"* has the etymological meaning of "cutting" or "smoothing" a piece of jade *(yü)* (see *Shuo Wen*). *"Li"* was

23. *(Continued)*

therefore later nominalized into a term for "pattern" or "order" in general from which the notion of reason, a function of ordering, has been derived. The term *"t'iao-li"* (the principles of order and reason) here refers to those orderings and patternings found in, but not separated from, things.

24. The "flow of the formation and transformation" *(hua-chih-liu)* refers to the unceasing but continuous creative activities of Heaven and Earth or the Way. See note 8, chapter 1.

25. I have explained the idea of *t'ien* in note 3, Tai Chên's Preface. The term *"ti"* (earth) appears in the *Book of Changes*, the *Record of Rites*, the *Tso Chuan* [Tso's Commentary on the *Spring and Autumn Annals*], and the *Book of Mencius*. The *Book of Changes* speaks of the Way of the *ti-tao* in its *"K'un wen-yen"* [Explanations and Judgments on the Triagram (or Hexagram) of *K'un*]; and the *Record of Rites* speaks of the *ti-ch'i* (the breath of the earth) in its *" Yüeh-ling."* In the high antiquity, *ti* as earth is an object of worship just as *t'ien* is; it is conceived as having the nourishing power and the power to sustain and to preserve. It is correlated with, and indeed complements, the power of *t'ien*, the power to generate and create. Since the time when the abstract ideas of the *yin* and *yang* were developed in the *Great Appendixes* of the *Book of Changes*, *ti* has been taken to represent the concrete form of *yin*, whereas *t'ien* has been taken to represent the concrete form of *yang*. See note 8, chapter 2.

26. See notes 3 and 4, chapter 1.

27. Proper in the sense of following the rules of propriety.

28. The term *"chung-ho"* is composed of *"chung,"* which refers to equilibrium or balance or the mean, and *"ho,"* which refers to harmony. Both concepts are found in the *Doctrine of the Mean*, which speaks of *chung* as a state where emotions remain unstirred and tranquility prevails; and of *ho* as a state where emotions are stirred, yet a balance and harmony is maintained in the stirred emotions. To attain *chung-ho* is to do everything in order and repose in the dynamic harmony of living forces. It is the ideal state of humanity. Both the word *"chung"* and

28. *(Continued)*
   the word *"ho"* are used in the earlier Classics such as the
   Book of Poetry, the *Book of Changes*, the *Book of Documents*,
   the *Commentary on the Spring and Autumn Annals*, and the
   Analects; they are used to represent the ideal acts of attaining
   centrality or states of perfection and harmony.

29. *Shêng-jên* is the sage, who, though a man, has supreme wisdom
   and supreme virtue and who therefore attains *jên* in its
   perfection, according to the Confucianists. *Shuo Wen*
   explains *"shêng"* as " *'t'ung'*—having profound understanding." In the *"Hsiang yin-chiu yi"* and the *"Record of Music"*
   in the *Record of Rites*, *shêng* is explained also as giving birth
   to or creating living things. Thus, a *"shêng-jên"* is a man who
   has profound understanding of everything and participates
   in the virtues of Heaven and Earth (*"Shêng-jên"* [The
   Sage], *Pei Hu T'ung* [Lectures in the White Tiger Hall]).
   It is in this sense that the term *"shêng-jên"* is used in the
   Great Appendixes of the *Book of Changes*. Generally, *shêng-jên*
   are conceived to exist in a Golden Age in the past. Thus,
   Confucius says: *"Shêng-jên*, I would no more see them"
   (*Analects*, 7.26). Mencius defines the state of *shêng* as one
   possessing greatness and transforming things *(ta êrh hua chih
   wei chih shêng)* (*Book of Mencius*, 7B.25). Furthermore, he
   identifies *shêng-jên* with historically known personages such
   as Po Yi, Liu Hsia-hui, and K'ung Tzŭ and classifies
   shêng-jên into types of purity *(ch'ing)*, perseverance *(jên)*,
   harmony *(ho)*, and timeliness *(shih)*. (See the *Book of
   Mencius*, 5B.1; 7A.7B.) In the *Doctrine of the Mean*, *shêng-jên*
   is given as one who participates in the creative and preserving
   activities of Heaven and Earth.

30. According to *Shuo Wen*, *yin* is the dark side of a thing and *yang*
   is the bright side of a thing. (*"Yin"* is used to indicate the
   south side of a river and the north side of a hill; *"yang"*
   is used to indicate the north side of a river and the south side
   of a hill.) According to the *"Wu-yi"* and the *"Hung Fan"*
   [Great Norm] in the *Book of Documents*, *yin* means the silent
   or the deep; in the *Book of Poetry*, *yin* is the shade, and *yang*,
   the sun. In the *Great Appendixes*, *yin* and *yang* refer to the
   two mutually complementary forces or principles of the
   process of the Way. *Yin* is the feminine, the receptive and the

41. The term "*tê*" here refers to the essence of things and men, the potential for development and growth. It is the root for every specific nature that is proper to the specific classes of things. That is why faith *(hsin)* is referred to as an outstanding virtue *(tê)* of men. See note 21, chapter 1.

42. The reason for the different desires in men and things lies in their having different endowments and capacities.

43. "Common share" is a translation of "*ta-kung*," which stands for "a common property of things." In this context, goodness is not merely something that things share in common in their natures but the ultimate form that things can be expected to fulfill when their natures are developed.

44. That is, to explain the nature of man and the world as derived from the Way, one has to have a deep and close knowledge of man and the world in their intimate relation to the Way.

45. See note 4, Tai Chên's Preface.

46. The question here is intended to indicate that every virtue can be regarded as a branching of *jên*. See also note 2, chapter 1.

47. Benevolence or *jên*, metaphysically speaking, is the principle of creating and preserving all lives. See note 2, chapter 1.

48. *Shuo Wen* explains "*yüan*" as "beginning." *Yüan* is also the capacity of creative activity, namely, the capacity of originating things. It represents an important metaphysical nature of *jên* in the explanation of the *ch'ien-kua* in the *Book of Changes*. *Yüan* is listed as the first and primordial virtue of *ch'ien* (the creative principle), followed by *hêng* (prosperity), *li* (furthering), and *chêng* (persevering).

49. This passage refers to the virtue of *hêng* (pushing through) as discussed in the explanation of the *ch'ien-kua* in the *Book of Changes*. This virtue, together with the virtues of *yüan* (see note 48, chapter 1), *li* (see note 50, chapter 1), and *chêng* (see note 52, chapter 1), composes the four cardinal metaphysical attributes of the Way or the four features of the attributes of the Way.

50. The term "*li*" refers to the beneficial accomplishment of the operation of the Way. See also note 48, chapter 1.

51. The criteria of order and reason are the same as those of the principles of order and reason.

52. The term *"chêng"* refers to the constancy and regularity of things. Obviously, by identifying *yüan, hêng, li,* and *chêng* with *jên, yi, li,* and *chih* respectively, we can see, on the one hand, the metaphysical significance of our ethical virtues, and the ethical significance of the metaphysical attributes, on the other. See also note 48, chapter 1.

53. Here "blood and breath" *(hsüeh-ch'i)* refers to the physical nature of the desires and feelings of a man; "intelligence and mind" *(hsin-chih)* refers to the higher mental faculties of man. See also note 15, chapter 1.

54. The term *"ch'iao"* (skill) refers to the capacity or skill of a man developed out of his natural endowments or training. That the *ch'iao* is a product related to the desires and feelings is because man has to learn or develop certain skills to express or satisfy his desires and feelings.

55. See note 16, chapter 1.

56. The heavenly principle here refers to the nature of the Way of Heaven and Earth.

57. The term "nature of Heaven" used here comes from the *Record of Rites* (see note 56, chapter 1). Whereas the Neo-Confucianists bifurcate human nature into the nature of Heaven *(yi-li-chih-hsing)* and the nature of physical desires *(ch'i-chih-chih-hsing)*, Tai Chên argues that no such bifurcation is in fact possible.

58. Here again, the necessity in human nature refers to what is potentially complete or perfect in human nature. See notes 7 and 40, chapter 1. I have followed James Legge in translating this passage. See Legge's translation of the *Book of Poetry,* 541.

59. *Book of Mencius,* 7B.24. In this paragraph, Mencius contrasts the concept of *ming* (necessity) and the concept of *hsing* (nature). From the standpoint of necessity, *ming,* as necessity, is different from *pi-jan,* the necessary. Both notes 40 and 58, chapter 1, refer to *pi-jan* as an ideal form or an ideal goal, whereas *ming* as used by Mencius in this passage refers to the

59. *(Continued)*

natural bodily desires, which are given to man and which have their natural function. It would be bad, according to Mencius, for man to indulge in or exaggerate his natural function at the expense of virtue. But Mencius does not deny that what is given to man is also a part of his nature. He is concerned about the distinguishing of this part of man's nature from that other part, which he calls *hsing* and which he feels man should develop, cultivate, and refine or perfect consciously. Both parts of man's nature are good, but *ming* is good to the extent that it is preserved as the basis of life, whereas *hsing* is good to the extent that it is cultivated as the guiding principle of life. The sense of necessity for *ming* has already been mentioned (see note 6, chapter 1). The latter sense refers to the limitations of what is given in human existence or other things.

60. The term "uprightness" *(chih)* refers to the balance and the mean of nature. Compare this with notions of equilibrium and harmony discussed in note 28, chapter 1.

61. This paragraph makes clear the metaphysical basis of human nature and human virtue. The Way of Man and the cultivation of human nature are essentially the same thing. They are sanctioned by what is given in man by Heaven. What also needs to be pointed out here is that the word "instruction" *(chiao)* also carries a connotation of the word "education."

62. A perfect development of goodness consists in achieving the fundamental virtues *(jên, li, yi)* and a harmony among them. In fact, it is natural that if the development or performance of one virtue prevents or contradicts that of another, then the virtue in question should not be considered virtue at all. Compare notes 9 and 11, chapter 1.

63. The translation of this passage is a modification of James Legge's translation (Legge's *Chinese Classics*, 313).

64. All these refer to the Confucian doctrine of the graded love and reverence. Having a certain graded love and reverence depends upon considerations of situations, relationships, and worth. The graded love and reverence are the bases for the various kinds of rules of propriety between various kinds of human relationships.

65. Here the term *"ch'ien"* refers to the force and function of *yang* (i.e., the masculine or creative, inceptive, rectifying, and ordering force and function) in the process of the activity of the Way of Heaven; *"k'un"* refers to the force and function of *yin* (i.e., the feminine or receptive, preserving, and conforming force and function) in the process of the activity of the Way of Heaven. Specifically, the words *"ch'ien"* and *"k'un"* refer to two principal trigrams ☰, ☷ ☷ or hexagrams ䷀, ䷁ ䷁ in the original texts of the *Book of Changes*. The terms *"yi"* (easiness) and *"chien"* (simplicity) are used in the *Book of Changes* to characterize the main capacities of *ch'ien* and *k'un* as two forces in the process of the activity of the Way. A man who attains these two capacities of the Way of Heaven will be called a sage *(shêng-jên)*, and a sage, as conceived by the *Book of Changes*, is a man who fully develops his nature and who can participate in the creative and preservative activities of the Way of Heaven.

66. See note 65, chapter 1.

67. The Chinese sentence reads: *"yi-chih tsê yü-ch'in."* *"Yü ch'in"* means "having something close to [him]." It seems natural to assume that something close to [him] in one's pursuit of knowledge is truth.

CHAPTER 2

1. The word *"ch'i"* (vital nature) literally means "breath," or "air," and it has a radical denotation of "clouds." It has occurred in both the Confucian Classics and the Taoist Classics. It has gained the meaning of a dynamic invisible element or reality of all things. It is used to explain the formation and transformation of things. Many modern Chinese philosophers, including Fung Yu-lan and Carsun Chang, interpret *"ch'i"* in terms of the Aristotelian matter or material force. But such an interpretation of *ch'i* is misleading because *ch'i* is not conceived to imply a sense of substantiality. In fact, the interpretation of *ch'i* as material force is somehow misleading, for it unnecessarily suggests something such as a "nonmaterial force." In the Classics, *ch'i* is used as the force or power that can give rise to life and things within shapes but remains immensely and permanently dynamic. It should be

1. *(Continued)*

   considered, therefore, a unique concept in the Chinese philosophy and should be best interpreted as something fundamental for the formation and transformation of the Way. Here the rendition of *ch'i* as vital nature indicates the life-giving property of *ch'i* as such. It can perhaps be translated also as "vital force."

2. See note 17, chapter 1.

3. Here, "the way of living" refers to both the overt way of conduct and the guiding principle of the conduct of man. The sage is a man whose way of conduct is always guided by virtue and by the sagacious understanding of the Way of Heaven.

4. The way of a sage, of course, is not just dissociated from the Way of Heaven and Earth; it is illuminated by the Way of Heaven and Earth.

5. The mean here is the natural balance or harmony that the vital nature and spirit of man possesses when they are normally and perfectly developed and maintained. The loss of this balance or harmony causes the amissness of man's vital nature and spirit.

6. The artificiality and derangement in one's spirit or mind surely lead to the falsification of the principles of reason in things and the disorder in one's conduct in relation to other men.

7. The sentence *"huo yü tê"* can also be translated as "those who are confused about virtues." For the word *"huo"* could mean: "have doubts about," "be confused about," or both. In the present context, it could mean both.

8. The word *"shên"* (spirit) refers to the refined part of one's nature that is not detached from the vital nature of man. To cultivate or nourish one's spirit shall be more conducive to a rational guiding of life than it is to cultivate or nourish one's vital nature.

9. The term "nature" here refers to the whole nature of a man.

10. The analogy of the beclouding of the sky indicates that the cultivating of one's spirit will reveal the deep capacity man's nature has toward virtue and good life. Cf. note 2, chapter 3.

11. The knowledge of the heavenly virtue *"t'ien-tê chih-chih"* here refers to the innate reflective knowledge of man regarding his ethical nature and rational origin. This is to be contrasted with his awareness of bodily desires.

12. Although one's knowledge of the heavenly virtue is apparently similar to what Ch'eng Yi and Chu Hsi call *"t'ien-ti chih hsing"* (the nature of Heaven and Earth) or *"yi-li chih hsing"* (the nature of righteousness and reason), it is not to be contrasted with the physical desires and natural temperaments of man; because the latter, like the former, is rooted in human nature. Tai Chên's point here is that one need not suppress the latter to advance the former, contrary to the teachings of the Sung Neo-Confucianists.

13. The term *"yi"* (righteousness), besides being a principle of righteousness, can be considered an innate capacity of man to do the right things or to follow righteousness, because, as we have seen, for Tai Chên, *yi* is one of the three main given goodnesses—*yi, jên, li*—in the nature of Heaven and the nature of man.

14. The phrase "five colors" refers to blue, yellow, red, white, and black. The reference to the five colors first appears in the *Hung Fan* [Great Norm] in the *Shu Ching* [Book of Documents]. The "five sounds" refers to the basic five notes of Chinese classical music. The five smells and the five tastes are mentioned in the *Li Chi* [Record of Rites].

15. The Way, as conceived here by Tai Chên, is what comes naturally in the formation of things. Cf. notes 3 and 4, preface.

16. *"Chih"* (knowing), when fully developed and cultivated to the utmost, will be so refined that it will penetrate into the subtlest movements of the Way of Heaven. At this stage, *chih* is considered by Tai Chên as the power of supreme intelligence or the power of perfect understanding; and it is called *shên-ming* (supreme illumination). Cf. note 17, chapter 1.

17. Here the term *"tao-yi"* (righteous disposition) can also be explained as the norms and capacity for action in accordance with the principles of righteousness that follow from the

17. *(Continued)*
     Way. This, according to Tai Chên, shows the presence of an a priori knowledge of virtue in us as derived from Heaven.

18. Benevolence *(jên)*, as we have noted (see note 2, chapter 1), is an all-comprehending virtue. For Tai Chên, not only does it serve as the basis and the ideal perfection for all other virtues such as righteousness and propriety but also actually manifest itself in the normal and harmonious functioning of physical desires and sense organs.

19. See note 7, chapter 1.

20. The term *"Chuan"* refers to the *Tso Chuan* [Tso's Commentary on the *Spring and Autumn Annals*].

21. According to *Shuo Wen* [On Words], *hun* is the male breath *(yang-ch'i)* and *p'o* is the female spirit *(yin-shên)*. Tzŭ Ch'an in *Tso's Commentary on the* Spring and Autumn Annals says: "The initial being of a man's life is *p'o*. When *p'o* is born, the *yang* part of *p'o* is called *hun*." In one place in the same work, *"hun"* is defined as "the spirit clinging to shape" *(fu-hsing chih-ling)*, whereas *"p'o"* is defined as "the spirit clinging to the vital nature" *(fu-ch'i chih-ling)*. Thus, they are two contrasting aspects of the spirit or soul *(ling)*. It might be suggested that the distinction between *hun* and *p'o* is made by Tai Chên entirely on a verbal level, owing to the Chinese penchant for coupling things *(tui-ou)*. The answer is that the distinction is probably based on the metaphysical principle of the complementary and opposite relation between the *yin* and the *yang*.

22. The term *"shên"* here refers to the *hun* of a man, and the term *"ling"* refers to the *p'o* of a man. See slso note 21, chapter 1.

23. See note 31, chapter 1.

24. The compound term *"hun-p'o"* (souls) again refers to the subtle functions and activities of Heaven and Earth. See note 21, chapter 1.

25. Here the phrase "the form and color" refers to the bodily organs and their sensible forms.

26. This is because of the individuating and ordering functions of the Way of Heaven. The restriction and limitation of the nature of an individual thing owing to the Way is called *ming* (necessity). See note 11, chapter 1.

27. The original text runs thus: *"ch'ü-ch'i-wei, pu-pao-ch'i-shih."* This sentence implies that man is capable of destroying living things. This may not necessarily be bad since man has to do this for the purpose of achieving a better human order that manifests the Way.

28. Compare my translation with James Legge's in his *Chinese Classics*, pp. 324–26.

29. Compare my translation with James Legge's in his *Chinese Classics*, pp. 326–27.

30. The original sentence reads: *"fei-ch'i-shu-hsi-yü-yi-chê-yeh."* Considered as a whole sentence without punctuation break, its translation is as given in the text. But one might break the sentence at the word *"shu,"* and thus translate it as "this is not due to his nature, but this is the result from being trained in proper behavior." This translation is exactly contrary to the original translation. This newly suggested reading of the sentence, however, is not justified in the light of the subsequent context, for Tai Chên, following Mencius, is arguing here for the innate goodness and the native knowledge of doing right that is innate in man.

31. The original text reads: *"k'o-chieh-chih shih-yü-shê-yeh."* In other words, we can induce an uncultured person to perceive and appreciate the principles of righteousness through the functioning of his native reason.

32. It is assumed here, of course, that the desire for wisdom would bring about efforts to achieve wisdom and that an untiring effort would lead to success.

33. See the chapter concerning *hsing-shan* in the *Mêng Tzǔ* (Book of Mencius), 6A.

34. *Great Norm, Book of Documents.*

35. This quotation not only shows Mencius' belief in the original goodness of human nature but also his belief in the innate knowledge of the goodness in human nature.

36. Tai Chên here refers to those who hold doctrines essentially different from the orthodox philosophy of Confucius, predominantly the Egoists of the Yang Chu school and the Mohists of the Mo Ti school, whose doctrines Mencius regarded as leading to a rejection of the status of the ruler and that of the father.

37. For the controversy between Kao Tzŭ and Mencius, see the *Book of Mencius*, 6A.

38. Here, I follow Legge's translation in his *Chinese Classics*.

39. Here, a syllogism is used implicitly: Since men have similar nature, and since there is no doubt that a sage has innate goodness and that a sage is a man, men are all innately good.

40. This is because the principles of reason and righteousness are ingrained in human nature just like some organic habits of men of which men may not be aware in their living.

41. Tai Chên's argument is this: That we do not naturally know that *li* and *yi* are something inherent in our nature should support the belief that *li* and *yi* must be so ingrained in human nature to entail that fact. But Tai Chên's argument here is obviously invalid. What he is trying to say is simply that human nature is good and that we do not know and yet can know that it is good.

42. This refers to the Neo-Confucianist conception of *li* (principle or reason). See my introduction and note 23, chapter 1.

43. For a discussion of Tai Chên's criticisms of the Neo-Confucian philosophy of *li*, see my Introduction.

44. That is, the mind has the function of realizing the structure of things on the basis of man's sensible perception.

45. "Natural endowments" is a translation of the term *"ts'ai-chih."* It refers to the native ability or inherent capacities in a thing. See note 13, chapter 1.

46. That is, they have no self-control and cannot guide the development of their natures in accordance with the highest principles of the Way of Heaven.

47. The natural tendencies of a man is *naturally* checked by his reason and by his native sense of righteousness. This is why even natural tendencies can be said to be good.

48. See note 31, chapter 1.

49. See the *Book of Mencius*, 6A. 3.

50. For Hsün Tzŭ's view, see Burton Watson's translation of *Hsün Tzŭ* [Writings of Hsün Tzŭ] (New York: Columbia University Press, 1963), chapter on *"Hsing O"* [On Human Nature Being Evil], pp. 157–71.

51. In the sense that he is not at rest because he cannot prevent himself from having desires.

52. *"Hai-tao"* (harm the Way) means "prevent the Way from being realized by man and from prevailing in human society."

53. Desires and feelings are considered bad according to the Sung Neo-Confucianists.

54. Here, Tai Chên draws the Taoist theoretical consequences of Kao Tzŭ's doctrine of human nature.

55. The term *"tzŭ-jan"* refers to what is naturally endowed in a man. But what is naturally endowed in a man is capable of developing into perfection, which is called the *pi-jan* in a man. See notes 40 and 66, chapter 1.

56. This is a restatement of Mencius' view that men may lose their goodness under corrupting circumstances. See note 7, chapter 1.

57. The original reads *"fang ch'i liang-hsin"* and *"shih ch'i pên-hsin,"* quoted from the *Book of Mencius*, 6A. 8; 6A. 10.

58. That is, until the nature of a man is completely lost, he may exercise himself to recover it.

59. Compare James Legge's translation in his *Chinese Classics*. Here Mencius describes the possible recovery of man's original goodness.

60. In Mencius' use of the term *"ch'i"* (vital nature), the more *ch'i* a man has, the more righteousness he will develop in his nature. In fact, Tai Chên's argument here is obviously

60. *(Continued)*

invalid. Apart from the argument, what he is trying to say here is simply that human nature is good and that we do and can know that it is good.

61. Here, "the greater part of a man's nature" refers to the function of mind; the smaller part, to the function of sense.

62. See note 22, chapter 1.

63. *Chung Yung* [Doctrine of the Mean]. The virtue of sincerity *(ch'êng)* entails the discovery of the innate goodness in man's nature and insures the development of man's nature into perfection, which is here referred to as *ming* (the enlightenment of intelligence). *Ming* is also "the full grasping of truth and the attainment of the Way"; hence, a virtue of a sage.

64. The *Doctrine of the Mean*. The virtue of *ming* in the sense of grasping truth and attaining the Way will necessarily lead to a sincere mind that encompasses the knowledge of goodness in man.

65. Lao Tan refers to Lao Tzŭ of the *Tao Tê Ching* (Book of Lao Tzŭ *or* The Way and Its Power); Chuang Chou refers to Chuang Tzŭ of the *Chuang Tzŭ* [Writings by Chuang Chou]. Both are classical Taoists, one of the sixth century B.C. and the other of the third century B.C.

66. Yü was the minister of state in the reign of the sage-king Shun, of the classical golden past. But he was later elected to be the successor of Shun and became a sage-king himself.

CHAPTER 3

1. The word "*ssŭ*" (selfishness) has been used in the Classics such as the *Shu Ching* [Book of Documents], the *Li Chi* [Record of Rites], the *Tso Chuan* [Tso's Commentary on the *Spring and Autumn Annals*], the *Yi Li*, and the *Lun Yü* [Analects]. The word refers to a private self or something or person belonging to someone. This meaning is often contrasted with that of the term "*kung*" (the public or belonging to the public that is identified with a society, or an organization, or a state).

2. The word *"pi"* (beclouding) used in the *Record of Rites* refers to covering, hiding, or sheltering. Later, it gained the meaning of separation and obstruction. The obstruction of mind results in the unclarity of ideas and the prejudice of opinion. It is in this sense that this term, translated as "beclouding" here, is used by Tai Chên.

3. This is so because the man then will not cultivate himself into goodness and perfection. It is recognized by Confucianists not only that a man should pay attention to his own needs and feelings but also that a man should satisfy his own needs and feelings of other men at the same time.

4. This reference concerns the strengthening of the virtue of *shu* (compassion), which is the capacity of thinking of other men's needs and feelings in terms of one's own needs and feelings; hence, the capacity of helping others to achieve satisfaction and well-being.

5. Again, these virtues are related to the basis of goodness. See notes 2, 3, 4, chapter 1.

6. Wisdom *(chih)*, benevolence *(jên)*, and courage *(yung)* are the three cardinal virtues of a superior man as stated in the *Analects*. Here, benevolence is to be understood in the sense of compassion or love, not in the broad sense of the creative and comprehensive productiveness.

7. Loyalty *(chung)* involves personal commitment to goodness. To be loyal to oneself, one must be able to develop oneself into perfection as much as possible.

8. That *jên* (benevolence) is called the prototype of all virtues is because *jên* is continuous with the metaphysical power of the formation and transformation of the Way; it is a principle of unity.

9. The term *"yi"* (easiness) refers to the essential feature of performing the function of the masculine or the creative force of the Way, whereas the term *"chien"* (simplicity) refers to the essential feature of performing the function of the feminine or the receptive force of the Way. Therefore, both *yi* and *chien* can be said to be the second-order features of the *yang* and *yin* of the Way. They indicate how the *yang*

9.   *(Continued)*

and *yin*—and for that matter how the Way—proceed, achieve, penetrate, and comprehend in unity, with facility; and how they are universally intelligible, even though their functions are also at the same time profound and unlimited. That loyalty resembles easiness and compassion resembles simplicity implies that loyalty and compassion are immense and profound real virtues of men, which should be followed and cultured. See also note 65, chapter 1.

10.   See note 9, chapter 3.

11.   For the contrast between opinion or belief *(chih)* and wisdom or true understanding or prudence *(chih)*, see note 18, chapter 1.

12.   The reason is that each man will follow his own subjective opinions, which are bound to conflict. The way of man is to discover the objective and universal elements in a man's nature and to cultivate them toward universal goodness.

13.   Then they will be self-contented regarding their virtuous self-cultivation. The limited and superficial achievements of virtues should not be taken as exhausting or revealing the great profundity of the Way of Heaven.

14.   The connotation of this contrast is clear: A man may not spontaneously make effort to improve himself, but he may be changed or transformed by external influences from other persons or from inner or outer circumstances.

15.   This passage urges that even small things are more significant and influential than big things. In the *Yi Ching* [Book of Changes], there is the doctrine that things in the world develop from small beginnings. Therefore, to control small beginnings is to control a whole and large-scale development and its results.

16.   Here, the self-control and self-examination to achieve virtue are emphasized. This, of course, also presupposes the importance of the individuality and the individual worth of a person, independently of a society but in direct response to Heaven.

17. It is assumed that when a person is alone, he is in perfect control of himself. His decision would be a decision of free will and a discovery of his own nature. Confucianists believe that a man can be truly responsible for his actions.

18. The *chung* (equilibrium) of mind is the balance of mind before things stir it; the *ho* (harmony) of mind is the balance of mind after it receives stimulation from things. The *chung* is a static state, whereas the *ho* is a dynamic state because it involves a process of harmonization *(chung-chieh)* or hitting the mark, thus, reaching due proportions of response. They are the two main illustrations of the *Doctrine of the Mean* or the principle of the mean. See also note 28, chapter 1.

19. The word *"chüeh"* that has been translated as "feelings" here literally means "perceptions."

20. See note 16, chapter 2, for explanation. The man himself and others will be transformed.

21. The whole passage can be taken not only as a description but also as a prescription of how a superior man should betake himself to self-cultivation.

22. That is to say, all men are endowed with some natural reason or natural light that is essential for further development. That men do have some natural reason or natural light should ensue from the fact that human nature has innate goodness.

23. Being unselfish is also a natural consequence of the innate goodness of human nature.

24. This passage refers to the profound good and stable nature of man achieved through intense self-cultivation.

25. This is the famous doctrine of self-cultivation by extension and comprehension in the Confucian philosophy.

26. The teaching of the great learning is embodied in the writing entitled the *Ta Hsüeh* [Great Learning], which is regarded traditionally as having been written by Tseng Tzŭ, the archdisciple of Confucius. This writing is incorporated as a chapter into the *Li Chi* [Record of Rites]. Modern scholars have dated it at the time of the middle of the fourth century B.C. or later.

27. This quotation is from the *Book of Changes;* hence, it refers to a specific hexagram of which it is in part an explanation or a comment. The hexagram to which it refers represents the combination of the earth above and the running water below.

28. That is, the natural desires of man signify the creative function of the Way.

29. That is, the father-son and the elder-younger brother relationships belong to those made possible by Heaven; hence, these relationships are not created by men or society.

30. That is, the relationship between husband and wife is one of complementation and cooperation.

31. This passage describes how closely and naturally related are the development and practice of virtues (*li* and *yi*), on the one hand, and the survival and well-being of a man in society, on the other.

32. Taken from the *"Kao T'ao Mo"* [Consultations of Kao T'ao] of the *Yü Hsia Shu* [Codes of Yü Hsia] in the *Book of Documents.* The term *"Yü Hsia"* refers to the kingdoms established by the sage-king Shun and the sage-king Yü. The *Codes of Yü Hsia* is held traditionally as records of sayings in the reigns of Shun and Yü.

33. *Ibid.*

34. *Ibid.*

35. *Ibid.*

36. The government is based on the observance of virtues of various kinds. It is known as government by virtue in the Confucian philosophy.

37. Mencius here describes a form of welfare state that is based on the so-called nine-square system of land distribution. The nine-square piece of land, having a shape looking like so ﹟, is to be cultivated by eight families, each of which owns a surrounding square of the center square. The center square belongs to the state.

38. This saying describes how the Way of Heaven can be realized in the state for the well-being of the people.

39. The term *"ta-kung"* (great public-mindedness) refers to the open spirit of justice of an unselfish man or to the principle of belonging to all. The *Evolution of Rites* in the *Record of Rites* says that "When the world reaches a great unity, then the government belongs to everyone in the world." This is a Confucian ideal of government by the people.

40. "The art of closing and opening" *(ho-p'i-chih-chi)* refers to the advantage-taking tricks or intrigues that a man may learn to use for doing evil things.

41. To use "the art of closing and opening" for doing evil things certainly is out of the order of the Way of Heaven, which functions only in accordance with the goodness of things.

42. *Judgment on the Seventh Hexagram Named Shih, Book of Changes.*

43. *Ibid.*

44. Beginning with this sentence and continuing on into the very end of this paragraph, Tai Chên apparently makes an implicit criticism of the management of some government officials or local officials whom he had known.

45. This poem reminds a ruler of his duty to benefit his people and to bring peace and justice to the kingdom of his rule in accordance with the Will of Heaven.

46. This poem suggests that those who rule the people are responsible for the well-being of the people.

47. The whole poem can be regarded as a metaphor concerning how a ruler of well-cultivated virtue may benefit the people.

48. The whole poem can be regarded also as a metaphor concerning the benevolent attitude of a virtuous ruler and his beneficent deeds.

Selected Bibliography

Freeman, Mansfield. "The Philosophy of Tai Tung-yüan," *Journal of the North China Branch of the Royal Asiatic Society* 64 (1933): 50–71.

Fung Yu-lan. *A History of Chinese Philosophy*, vol. 2. Translated by Derk Bodde. Princeton: Princeton University Press, 1953.

Hou Wai-lu. *Chung-kuo ching-shih ssŭ-hsiang shiao-shih* [A Short History of Modern Chinese Thought], vol. 1. Shanghai: The People's Publishing Co., 1947.

Hu Shih. *Tai Tung-yüan tê chê-hsüeh* [The Philosophy of Tai Tung-yüan]. Shanghai: The Commercial Press, 1927.

Tai-shih yi-shu [The Remaining Works of Mr. Tai]. An old text edited by K'ung Chi-han.

Tai Tung-yüan êrh-pai-nien shêng-jih chi-nien lun-wen chi [Tai Tuan-yüan, Essays in Celebration of the Two Hundredth Anniversary of His Birth Date]. Compiled by the Morning Times Press. Peking: 1924. This collection of essays includes: "Introduction," "Biography of Tai Tung-yüan," "Inquiry into the Bibliography of Tung-yüan's Writings and Works in Compilation and Textual Collation," and "The Philosophy of Tung-yüan," all of which by Liang Ch'i-ch'ao; "The Arithmetics and Astronomy of Tai Tung-yüan," by Ch'en Chan-yün; "Tai Tung-yüan in the History of Chinese Psychology," by Wang Cheng; "Tai Tung-yüan's Ideas about the *Book of Poetry*," by Wu Shih-ying; and "Tung-yüan's *Sequel to Brief Astronomical Studies* and *Sequel to Brief Astronomical Studies in T'ung Chih*," by Chou Liang-hsi.

Tai Tung-yüan Chi [Collection of Essays of Tai Tung-yüan].
Published originally by Tuan yü-chai; reprinted by the
Commercial Press. Shanghai: 1933.

Wing-tsit Chan. *A Source Book in Chinese Philosophy.* Princeton:
Princeton University Press, 1963.

Yüan Shan [Inquiry into Goodness], *Mêng Tzǔ tzǔ-yi shu-chêng*
[Commentaries on the Meanings of Terms in the *Book of
Mencius*], compiled by the Ancient Texts Press. Peking:
Ancient Texts Press, 1956.

Index